Back to Gridlock?

Back to Gridlock?

Governance in the Clinton Years

James L. Sundquist, Editor
Introduction by Hedrick Smith

THE BROOKINGS INSTITUTION
COMMITTEE ON THE CONSTITUTIONAL SYSTEM
Washington, D.C.

ISBN 0-8157-8233-0

Library of Congress Catalog Number 95-083186

9 8 7 6 5 4 3 2 1

Typeset in Times New Roman

Composition by Oakland Street Publishing
Arlington, Virginia

Printed by Kirby Lithographic Co.
Arlington, Virginia

Preface

On May 1, 1995, the Committee on the Constitutional System, the Brookings Institution, and the Council for Excellence in Government convened a conference in Washington, D.C., to discuss the effectiveness of the U.S. governmental system. The participants looked back on the experience of the first two years of the Clinton administration and ahead to the prospects for the next two years with the new Republican majorities in control of Congress.

The conference was designed as a successor to a similar meeting conducted in February 1993, at the outset of the Clinton administration, by the Committee on the Constitutional System and Brookings. Highlights of that discussion were condensed in a book, *Beyond Gridlock?,* published by Brookings. That conference focused on the question of whether a government in which both the executive and legislative branches were controlled by a single party—the Democrats—would function more successfully than the divided governments (with Republicans holding the presidency and Democrats controlling one or more houses of Congress) of the preceding twelve years.

The 1995 symposium brought together a similar group of distinguished observers of the national political scene—former high administration officials and members of Congress, Washington-based journalists, political scholars, and civic leaders—to address the question asked at the earlier meeting by reviewing the successes and failures of two years of unified government. Then the participants asked the new question posed by the return of divided government as the result of the 1994 midterm election: Would the conflict between a

Democratic administration and the Republican Congress mean a return to what during the Reagan and Bush years (and, before that, during most of Eisenhower's eight years and all of Nixon's and Ford's) was commonly termed "gridlock"? Hence the title of this book. Eighteen of the conference speakers have converted their presentations into chapters for *Back to Gridlock?*, and their contributions are gratefully acknowledged.

The conference could not have taken place without the dedicated efforts of Peter Schauffler, coordinator of the Committee on the Constitutional System since its formation, who worked tirelessly in planning and arranging the event, in consultation with Thomas E. Mann, director of the Governmental Studies program at Brookings, and under the general direction of Lloyd N. Cutler, co-chair of the committee. Jack Duvall gave helpful advice on the format of the conference and the selection of participants; Hedrick Smith, distinguished author, analyst, and commentator, skillfully moderated the proceedings. Robert Redd ably transcribed the conference proceedings, Nancy Davidson supervised the book's initial development, and Stephanie Selice helped the participants to convert spoken presentations into appropriate form for publication and edited the manuscript.

Financial support for the conference and related activities was provided by the Heinz Family Foundation, the USX Foundation, and the Dillon Fund.

James L. Sundquist

Contents

Participants

Howard H. Baker, Jr.
Partner, Baker, Donelson, Bearman & Caldwell. White House chief of staff to President Reagan, 1987–88. U.S. senator, Republican of Tennessee, 1967–85, and Senate majority leader, 1981–85.

Harold R. Bruno, Jr.
ABC News political director since 1978. Formerly chief political correspondent, *Newsweek.*

Becky Cain
President, League of Women Voters, and chair, League of Women Voters Education Fund. Representative/board member, the Committee on the Constitutional System and Citizens for Tax Justice, among others.

Lloyd N. Cutler
Co-chair, Committee on the Constitutional System. White House counsel to President Clinton, 1994, and President Carter, 1979–81.

Thomas J. Downey
Chair, Downey Chandler, Inc. U.S. representative, Democrat of New York, 1975–93. Member, Ways and Means Committee, and congressional adviser to SALT II and START negotiations.

Kenneth M. Duberstein
President, The Duberstein Group, Inc. Assistant to the president for legislative affairs, deputy chief of staff, and chief of staff to President Reagan, 1981–83, 1987–89. Director of congressional relations, General Services Administration, Nixon administration. Deputy undersecretary of labor, Ford administration.

Bill Frenzel
Guest Scholar, Governmental Studies program, Brookings Institution. U.S. representative, Republican of Minnesota, 1971–91.

Charles O. Jones
Hawkins Professor of Political Science, University of Wisconsin-Madison. Douglas Dillon Visiting Fellow, Governmental Studies program, Brookings Institution. Past president, American Political Science Association.

Thomas E. Mann
Director, Governmental Studies program and W. Averell Harriman Senior Fellow in American Governance, Brookings Institution. Former executive director, American Political Science Association.

Patricia McGinnis
President and chief executive officer, Council for Excellence in Government. Former deputy associate director, Office of Management and Budget.

Milton D. Morris
Vice President, Joint Center for Political and Economic Studies. Former senior fellow, Governmental Studies program, Brookings Institution.

Kevin P. Phillips
Editor-publisher, *American Political Report*, American Political Research Corporation. Author, *Arrogant Capital* (1994).

Robert D. Reischauer
Senior Fellow, Economic Studies program, Brookings Institution. Director, Congressional Budget Office, 1989–94.

Donald L. Robinson
Professor of government, Smith College. Research director, Committee on the Constitutional System. Author, *Government for the Third American Century* (1989).

Hedrick Smith
Television producer since 1986. *New York Times* reporter and editor, 1962–88; Moscow bureau chief, 1971–74, Washington bureau chief, 1976–79; chief Washington correspondent, 1979–85. Author, *The Power Game: How Washington Works* (1988).

James L. Sundquist
Senior fellow emeritus, Brookings Institution. Author, *Constitutional Reform and Effective Government* (rev. ed. 1992).

Robin Toner
New York Times correspondent, Washington bureau.

Vin Weber
Partner, Clark & Weinstock, Inc. Vice chair, Empower America. Senior fellow, Progress and Freedom Foundation. Co-chair, Domestic Strategy Group, Aspen Institute. Co-chair, Policy Forum, Humphrey Institute. U.S. representative, Republican from Minnesota, 1980–92.

Introduction

Hedrick Smith

This book is based on presentations made at a conference sponsored by the Brookings Institution, the Committee on the Constitutional System, and the Council on Excellence in Government that was held on May 1, 1995.

This was the second such conference, the first having been held in February 1993. At that point we were poised at the very beginning of the Clinton administration. The question was whether the emergence of a united government—that is, a government in the hands of one political party, with the White House, the House of Representatives, and the Senate all controlled by the Democrats—could operate more effectively than divided government that had confused and frustrated the voters, causing them to take out their frustration on President Bush and the Republicans in the White House in the previous election. We debated vigorously whether there should be reform of the system—from modest reforms such as campaign finance to major constitutional reforms such as party team tickets.

That conference resulted in a book, *Beyond Gridlock?*, published by Brookings. This book is its sequel.

The 1995 meeting marked another pivotal moment, more pivotal than we had expected when we planned it—a moment in which the Republicans have now restored divided government by taking control of the House of Representatives and the Senate while a Democratic president still occupies the White House.

The Republican takeover of Congress is certainly a seminal event that has not been matched in a generation. It is important not only because it marks the change of political control of the House of Representatives for the first time in forty years, but also because it represents in both substance and in institutional arrangements the most profound change in our political system since the New Deal and even before.

Substantively, of course, Speaker Newt Gingrich and his colleagues in the House, the newly elected Republicans, presented a challenge to the entire philosophy of the New Deal—the philosophy and principle of governmental activism—and they raised a brand new debate on the role of government on a whole range of issues.

In terms of constitutional arrangements, they also presented a fundamental challenge. Ever since Franklin Roosevelt in the early 1930s, we have assumed in America that the presidency was the pivot point of leadership, the driving force, of the American government. But as soon as this new Congress was sworn in, the center of gravity in the American government shifted to Capitol Hill, to the House of Representatives, and to Speaker Gingrich himself—an arrangement that is more reminiscent of the way American politics operated in the nineteenth century than most of the twentieth century.

This raised a question not only about substantive policy but also about whether American government can be driven and directed from Congress more effectively than from the White House. Would the Senate, and particularly Senate Republicans, go along with what the House Republicans sought to do in the Contract with America? And then, even more important perhaps, would the president go along? Would the House, the Senate, and the president form the kind of coalitions that would make American government work, or would gridlock return? Hence the title of this book. As of May 1995, it certainly was an open question.

The opening chapters look back at the record of the Clinton administration during its first two years. The next contributions examine what happened in the first one hundred days or so after the Republican takeover of Congress.

We then move into a wider debate about the state of affairs in the American political system: whether what has happened already is sufficient (changing parties, changing faces), or whether some much more fundamental changes are required to make our system work effectively.

Our look at the Clinton record focuses specifically on the budget

and on the health care reform package. But Thomas Mann asks a question at the very beginning that is important for examining not only Clinton's performance, but also the functioning of our political system as a whole: Was there an opportunity that Clinton and the Democrats could have seized and, as a result, performed well—or were they doomed in advance?

Responding to that question, Hal Bruno comments on the absence of discipline, respect, and fear among Democrats for each other and for the president. Mann himself talks about the constraints on Clinton. Robin Toner presents a detailed examination of the health care package, identifying the huge problems its supporters faced in attempting to get it through. Whether or not it was a good package to begin with, was there enough time? Was there enough coherence among the Democrats?

Robert Reischauer raises an even bigger question in his chapter on the budget struggles of the first Clinton years. Can something that large be passed without a bipartisan coalition or at least a method of policy formulation at the beginning of the process that wraps Congress and the president together? That would alter the usual notion that the president is the one who proposes and Congress disposes, by getting them started on the same sheet of music to begin with. Even the success of the budget package produced no great sense of achievement, because it was one that distributed pain, and that pain was politically costly to the president and the Democrats in the 1994 election. Ken Duberstein gives support to Reischauer's view, pointing out that Clinton was most successful, and looked most successful, when he was bipartisan, as in dealing with NAFTA, with GATT, and with the question of most favored nation status for China.

Of course, the writers who comment on Newt Gingrich and the Republican takeover of Congress lack the benefit of hindsight. But they are virtually unanimous in saying that the first one hundred days, at least from within the Beltway, looked like a very impressive performance—not only in terms of legislative results but also in the concentration of power in the Speaker, which gave him the ability to move the system and focus the agenda.

Speculating on what lies ahead, particularly on the fate of the Contract with America, writers inevitably differ, depending on their politics. Yet Democrat Tom Downey and Republican Bill Frenzel paradoxically both defend gridlock. In Downey's view, the Democrats should be about the business of opposing, not creating; they should seek gridlock in the next couple of years. That is what the Republicans did effectively in 1993–94, and it paid off politically in the November 1994 elections.

Ken Duberstein expresses confidence that the Republican package will move reasonably well because Newt Gingrich and Bob Dole both understand, as does Bill Clinton, that governing well is the best politics. On the other hand, Charles Jones predicts it will not work that way, and Bruno and Frenzel appear to share that opinion.

Looking broadly at the political system as a whole and at the mood of the country, Howard Baker and Lloyd Cutler discuss the age of anger and alienation. Baker is eloquent about the loss of the politics of civility. Not a man with a partisan ax to grind, he observes that the lack of civility and the animus between members of Congress and the White House, and among members of Congress across party lines, is very different from when he came to Congress in 1966. Today, Baker notes, a sense of enmity and a sharp edge are damaging the effectiveness of government and eroding the public's confidence in it. Cutler extends this point in writing of the growing animus between the people and the government, public mistrust of government, and the onus that is on public servants.

This theme recurs in many of the other chapters. Becky Cain finds it symptomatic that about 60 percent of the eligible voters did not vote in the 1994 election. Only 70 million people went to the polls, a turnout rate lower than that of the presidential election in 1992 and up just a bit from the previous off-year election of 1990. Pat McGinnis reports on public opinion polls sponsored by her organization that reflect the lowering of sights for the American dream. Only 15 percent of the people polled express confidence in the federal government, and I am sad to hear but not surprised that only 19 percent have confidence in the media. In all honesty, I think the media are part of the problem of alienation. On the same theme, Kevin Phillips notes that 57 percent of the people want a third party. Sixty to 65 percent of the people polled say Washington in 1995 is operating with politics as usual, the same in the spring of 1995 as in 1994.

A second theme running through many of the contributions is the enormous impact on the political system of changes that have taken place outside it. One is the end of the cold war, which means that presidents can no longer stand up and be strong, representing the nation against the communists. That was how the power and the image of the presidency could always be repaired over the last half-century, but it is no longer available to rally a weak president.

A second change is the development of a pervasive economic insecurity in the country. Pat McGinnis's polls suggest that more and more people are uneasy about their economic future. Milton Morris refers to the economic inequality in the country, the difficulties and strains arising from this social disparity, the lower economic aspirations. It is much easier to run a positive and effective democracy, he notes, when aspirations are high and rising, much more difficult when they are low, shrinking, or static. So the public alienation today consists not just of political disaffection, but also of economic disaffection and disconnection.

Finally, the authors talk about reform.

I am fascinated that Kevin Phillips, picking up from Lamar Alexander and Howard Baker, speaks of the notion of a citizen legislature: serve for six months, then get out of town.

Phillips discusses an array of ideas and trends: term limits, not only for politicians but also for lobbyists and journalists; the notion of direct democracy through national referenda as in New Zealand, Australia, and occasionally even in Great Britain; a suggestion that the two-party system simply will not last, that the Ross Perot phenomenon of 1992 will be repeated in some form or another, perhaps with a proliferation of candidates—a Perot or a Colin Powell for one part of the political spectrum, and a Jesse Jackson for another part of the spectrum. Charles Jones offers a very different view of the prospects of change. He foresees the same kind of system as we have now—muddling along, constantly adjusting, able to deal with new trends as they appear. Donald Robinson, who has been a spokesman for many of the major reforms considered by the Committee on the Constitutional System, has now evolved philosophically to the point where he is defending democracy as being most effective and responsive, and most likely to be supported, when carried out in local towns and villages. But how will village democracy work in Harlem or Watts? Is it sustainable as a system for the United States as a whole?

Finally, James Sundquist eloquently advocates one of the central proposals of the Committee on the Constitutional System—to do away with the midterm elections, allowing a longer breathing space for politicians, relieving the pressure on them to be immediately responsive to the next election, giving an opportunity for some cohesion, some momentum in policy, before letting the public make its judgment. Others among these writers—Vin Weber, Ken Duberstein, Bill Frenzel—would surely disagree. Frenzel, defending gridlock, cautions against veering in one direction and then another. Caution also comes from Morris, suggesting that this is an adjustable system, and even more from Jones, who notes that even the question of public disaffection was one that Felix Frankfurter mentioned sixty-five years ago.

Sixty-five years ago was 1930. If in fact the way we feel today about our government is the way people felt in 1930, that is not a good sign, but a very bad one. That year was just after the crash of 1929. If now a slow erosion in the economic situation has created a public mood similar to that of the Great Depression years, we should not be reassured but downright alarmed. We may have more to worry about than we thought.

In any case, the chapters that follow lay it all out. Some contributors think the system is going to be all right, that it will play well with a lot of the Republican Contract with America to be passed. Some think it will not play so well, but that demonstrates the effective working of the system in another way. Still others say no, the system is not working well enough, as reflected in the increasing alienation of the people and the prospect of a large third-party vote in the 1996 elections. That bodes a long-term trend that requires what Sundquist has called preventive maintenance applied to the governmental system.

By late 1995 and early in 1996 we will get our first clear look at the answer. What happens then will determine the vote in 1996. Given this clash of philosophies, the chances of public frustration are enormous unless the American government operates with surprising efficiency and coherence in the months to come.

United Government: A Democratic President and Congress (1993–94)

President Clinton and the Democratic Congress: Promise and Performance

Thomas E. Mann

The 1994 electoral earthquake left in its wake signs of a new political order, as Republicans swept control of the Congress, ending a forty-year drought in the House, and moved into a dominant position in states and regions across the country. For President Clinton it was a surprising and bitter defeat. Only two years earlier, basking in the glory of his own election victory, he had eagerly and confidently anticipated the legislative fruits of a return to unified party government. Yet now he faced a Republican Congress aggressively promoting its own policy agenda and intent on reversing many of his modest legislative accomplishments. What happened along the way? What was the promise of his administration? And how do we account for its performance?

Early in the Clinton presidency, it was possible to see the opportunities and the obstacles, the possibilities and the limits of his administration. On the one hand, there were serious obstacles facing the new united Democratic government. The president was elected with a fragile electoral base: he garnered 43 percent of the popular vote, and his party lost ten seats in the House of Representatives. Although congressional Democrats were more ideologically cohesive than in the days when the conservative coalition ruled Congress, there remained serious differences among them, especially on issues of taxes and social policy. Republicans were likely to be united in their opposition to major initiatives to increase the role of government.

Quite apart from ideology and partisanship, Congress had its own strong institutional interests in our separated system of government. The public was in an ugly mood—deeply divided over what needed to be done, cynical about the motivations of politicians, and skeptical about the government's ability to solve pressing problems. The problems themselves were enormously complex, and their solutions entailed substantial redistribution among citizens and economic interests as well as visible and immediate pain for ambiguous and uncertain long-term gains. And there were already signs of a stumbling start to the Clinton presidency, including a rocky transition from campaigning to governing and several well-publicized embarrassments in the first weeks after the inauguration.

Although it would be a mistake to underestimate these constraints, it was also important to recognize the favorable dynamics at work. These included the return of one-party government after an extended period of intensely polarized divided government, especially in an era of greater party unity and at a time the Democrats were desperate to demonstrate their ability to govern. The large freshmen class and the public impatience with business as usual were also thought to provide opportunities for successful governance.

To take advantage of this new dynamic, the president needed to fashion a mandate that was faithful to the central tenets of his campaign. This mandate had to be attentive to the real problems facing the country, persuasive to other members of the political community and to the public, and translatable into concrete proposals for government action. At the time I thought there were reasonable prospects that the president could meet that challenge and begin to develop a more constructive partnership with the Congress. My expectation was not that he would play a dominant role in dealing with Congress or that unified government would produce a bountiful legislative harvest; rather, that a sense of shared stakes and greater ideological compatibility between the two branches would facilitate a more productive relationship than had existed in the last two years of the Bush administration.

With the benefit of hindsight, we now see that even that modest forecast was overly optimistic. President Clinton has been in a constant state of political peril. The shortcomings of his administration in terms of organization, strategy, and personal style have been well chronicled, in two books published before the midterm elections by Bob Woodward and Elizabeth Drew as well as in scores of articles.

What we know is that the very high presidential support score during 1993—one President Clinton was so proud of pointing to as an indicator that he was the most successful president working with

Congress since Dwight Eisenhower—belied an exceedingly difficult though reasonably productive first year. The year was a roller coaster. There were early failures, including the political flap over gays in the military and the misjudgment on the economic stimulus bill, which led to the first of a series of partisan filibusters in the Senate that came to haunt the president throughout his first two years in office. But their were substantial victories as well. A major deficit reduction package (which though unrecognized by the public included a substantial tax cut for millions of Americans through an increase in the earned income tax credit) was adopted without a single Republican vote in either the House or Senate. The North American Free Trade Agreement was approved after an uphill struggle, one in which the president took on many of the core constituencies in the Democratic party and built a majority coalition with strong Republican support. Other legislative achievements included several leftovers from the previous congress (family leave and the motor voter registration bill) as well as the Brady gun control bill, aid to Russia, national service, and student loan reform.

There was no dramatic change in policy course during that first year, but some important and constructive achievements. Many key issues, including health and welfare reform, were deferred to 1994. And as that first year ended, the president was weakened by tentative foreign policy leadership and new assaults on his character from Paula Jones and the reemergence of Whitewater.

The second year ended on a disastrous note as the temporary but politically damaging setback on the crime bill, collapsing public support for national health reform, and the president's unpopularity emboldened the Republicans to adopt a scorched-earth strategy. They blocked virtually every piece of legislation at the end of the session (including those that enjoyed broad bipartisan support), which proved remarkably effective in convincing the American public that Bill Clinton and the Democrats were not competent to make Washington work. This was followed, of course, by the historic electoral defeat that relegated the Democrats to minority status in the House and Senate and marginalized the president.

How are we to understand this brief and unsuccessful episode of united party government? Was it a lost opportunity, or were this president and Congress doomed to failure?

If there was a bias toward failure, is the problem largely a function of our political institutions, our unique system of separated institutions competing for shared powers? Or is it more a result of other forces operating in society? The list of such forces is long. It begins with the decline of trust in government, the shift from the healthy skepticism Americans have always had toward their political leaders to a corrosive cynicism. Traumatic national events, economic insecurity, a fraying of the social fabric, and shifting patterns of media coverage of politics have contributed to a growing disillusionment with government and a resentment against those who run it—not the firmest base of public opinion on which to launch new government initiatives.

The president also faced a policy legacy that posed more constraints than opportunities. Large structural deficits prevented any positive-sum strategies in building coalitions for major policy change. Moreover, the loss of control over the budget—with mandatory spending programs dwarfing discretionary activities—diminished the ability of policymakers to change course. The end of the cold war brought uncertainty to international security and weakened domestic support for global engagement by the United States.

Another force complicating the task of governing was the growing ideological polarization among elites and activists and the political mobilization of economic and social interests. Increasingly, policymakers were pressed with extreme, nonnegotiable demands, making the search for accommodation elusive and daunting efforts to build a coalition from the center out.

President Clinton and the Democratic Congress were also attempting to govern during a "political time" that favored the opposition party. The party of the New Deal and its policy regime has been eroding over the last several decades; a collapse seemed imminent. It is not easy for the party in decline to revitalize its coalitional base while in power.

Finally, the gathering of plebiscitary pressures in American society has put a strain on the institutions of deliberative democracy. The communications revolution and the changing nature of the mass media have fueled a democratization of political information, a decline in mediating structures, and increasing demands by citizens to govern themselves more directly.

All of these forces certainly constrained the ability of a new Democratic president working with a Democratic Congress to build a record of success. As my colleague Bert Rockman recently framed the issue: Could the first two years of the Clinton presidency been done differently? The answer is yes. Could they have been done better? Almost certainly yes. Would doing so have mattered a great deal? Here the answer is much less certain. Given public cynicism, the policy legacy, ideological polarization, political time, and the rise of plebiscitary forces, it is not obvious that a more clearheaded and competent administration would have produced a substantial success in these first two years.

Did Clinton pass up alternative strategies for building majority coalitions in Congress and in the country? There was no shortage of pundits advising less ambitious, more centrist, and more bipartisan approaches in dealing with Congress, ones that took account of the fragile political base on which the president and Democrats in Congress were operating. It is undeniable that it would have been better for Bill Clinton to conceptualize his presidency with a more sober view of the narrowness of his electoral mandate, of the difficulty of steering our separated system and the necessity of adjusting his agenda and his style to the resources and constraints he faced. Such an adjustment would very likely have improved the performance of his administration.

And yet what at first glance seems an obvious strategy is in reality not so attractive. It is not easy to abandon one's modest political base in search of a new majority under conditions of extreme ideological polarization. Nor is it a simple matter to overcome shortcomings of personal style that are fully integrated parts of one's whole political personality.

But whatever the constraints on adjusting to the conditions of early 1993, the dramatic results of the 1994 elections have transformed those conditions, requiring another adjustment of strategy and tactics on the part of the president. As initiative has flowed to Capitol Hill under the daring leadership of Speaker Newt Gingrich, providing an episode of governance in the House more akin to a parliament than to our separated system, President Clinton has had to search for ways of making a political virtue out of a return to divided government. Unlike his leadership posture at the beginning of his presidency, Bill Clinton must now sing the praises of the Madisonian system whose checks and balances force moderation in the agenda of the new majority in Congress.

Recent critics of American government have bemoaned its proclivity for sluggishness and stalemate and entertained various constitutional and statutory changes that would strengthen the executive and concentrate power within the system. Many of the institutional changes embraced by the Republican majority in Congress—term limits, a balanced budget amendment, a line-item veto, reductions in congressional staff, limits on seniority, and strengthened party leadership—move in that direction. It will be interesting to see if the prospect of a unified Republican government after the 1996 elections, intent on using new power arrangements to pursue an ambitious conservative policy agenda, will lead to a renewed appreciation by reformers and public alike for our unique system of deliberative democracy.

A Political
Observer's View

Harold R. Bruno, Jr.

For those of us committing journalism today, the Republican takeover of Congress was the biggest upheaval we have seen in politics—much greater than when parties switch control of the White House. The last time it happened, forty years ago, as Rick Smith was careful to point out, I was a police reporter in Chicago and thinking about other things besides national politics.

The Republican gains went far beyond the House and Senate; they also included control of the statehouses. For the first time since 1970, there are more Republican than Democratic governors, and a tremendous gain in the state legislatures. Republican governors now are in charge of nine of the ten largest states. There are fourteen states where the Republicans have control not only of the governorship but of both houses of the state legislature. This means that the foundation of Democratic political power was knocked out from under them when they lost the House and the statehouses. In the past, the Democrats could lose the presidency, they could even lose the Senate for six years, but they still had that base of the House of Representatives plus the statehouses.

So how did this happen? As a political reporter I would divide it into two parts: the performance of the Clinton Administration, and the performance of the Democratic Congress. Then match those problems against the mood of the country. The result is this political upheaval.

First, the performance of the Clinton Administration: there arose a perception of incompetence and inability to govern. In the early stages it reminded me of Casey Stengel when he was managing the young

New York Mets. Stengel turned around in desperation in the clubhouse one day and said, "Does anybody here know how to play this game?" In the early stages of the Clinton administration it seemed as if nobody did. Even when they did the right thing, it was done in a clumsy way. They were very slow to organize their government, too many appointments got in trouble, and they were unable to shake the president's personal problems. Whitewater was badly handled—in fact, it could be a textbook case on how not to handle a problem in the White House.

This meant that questions persisted about the President's character. There was a chaotic management style that seemed to be undisciplined, a constant crisis atmosphere. The result is that members of the Clinton administration never got credit for some of their accomplishments, and the president began to lose credibility. The approval ratings went down and the disapproval ratings went up, and while they fluctuated over the last two years, it has been predominately a downhill trend.

When a President takes office, he is given what I call a "bank account of credibility," and he either draws on it or adds to it, depending on what happens. We have seen presidents who went bankrupt; they overdrew on their credibility accounts. The Clinton administration is not there at this point. But they have come close and things have to change, or they will have lost all credibility.

As a result, the administration did not get credit for things that turned out right. No matter what caused it, the economy improved. The budget deficit actually did start to go down. The problem is most people just did not feel good about it. The psychology of the economy is still negative. In politics it's the psychology of the economy that counts, because average Americans do not walk around turning over economic indicators in their minds. They are concerned about their own job security and their own savings, and there seems to be a lack of confidence in the economy.

I do not want to tread on ground that Robin Toner is going to cover, so I will just say this about health care: it became the big test for the Clinton administration, and they failed. The task force tried to do too much, too fast. They would not listen. Members of Congress who should have been involved from the very start were not, and the result was a political disaster.

Part of the question is, what caused the Clinton administration's problems? I think the first big mistake is that members of the administration came into Washington looking for a fight. They wanted to fight with Congress, which was their own party. They wanted to fight with the Washington establishment to show that they were "outsiders." And the result is that some of the most talented, experienced people in the Democratic Party—both in Washington and around the country— were never a part of the Clinton administration. Washington is a place that has to be managed. It is like an old camp follower; it surrenders to whoever wins. You have to take it over and run it. Instead, the Clinton people wanted to fight with Washington, and they left out the people who knew how to make the place work.

They also wanted to fight with us, the news media, which is not difficult. Usually it takes about six months before the bitter fighting starts, but the Clinton Administration went into the bunkers the day after inauguration.

As for the Clinton White House, I think the president deserves credit for the effort to have diversity on his team—to have an administration that "looks like America."

When you look at the men and women in the Clinton Administration, you see that most went to Ivy League schools. The Clinton people all come from the same background and think the same. Many were young and inexperienced. One of the great adventures with the early Clinton administration came when you had to call the White House. You tried to avoid it. Getting through was problem number one. Problem number two, if you got through, was to find the person you were trying to reach, and if he or she was not there, leaving a message—which was like sending a note out to sea in a bottle. I think what they need more than anything else is a handbook on good manners and the importance of returning calls.

Coupled with the administration's problems was the performance of the Democratic Congress. With a president in the White House and Democrats in control of Congress, there were great expectations, which they did not live up to. There was no party discipline. The Democrats would not follow their own leadership or the president. There was no respect, no fear, no confidence in the leadership on the Hill or at the White House.

I think health care, with all the plans proposed, was a good example of legislation by mob action. It was the Republicans who had to save the President on NAFTA, and then they saw the opportunity and turned obstructionist. In the final days of the 103d Congress, they simply would not allow anything to pass. They got away with it, and the public just didn't seem to care.

Going into the midterm election campaign, the Democrats were soft, fat, and smug. The Republicans were mean, fat with money, and hungry. The country was angry, frustrated, and fed up. The issues were crime, welfare, taxes, bad schools, immigration, and no confidence in the economy or the government. The anti-incumbent mood turned anti-Democratic, and the proof is that not a single Republican incumbent lost, whether it was a House, Senate, or governor's race.

A midterm election always is a referendum on a president, and this one it turned anti-Clinton. They could not fire him, so they fired his party.

The Republicans ran a clever and effective campaign. It was well put together and well financed. It was nationalized. I think Haley Barbour, Phil Gramm, Bill Paxton, and Newt Gingrich deserve a lot of credit for the campaign they delivered. They made the president the issue, hung him around the neck of every Democrat, and forced every Democrat to either defend him or run away—and most chose to run away. In any midterm election there always are isolated places where the president is not welcome to campaign for members of his own party. In this election there were only a few places where he was welcome. In most places they did not want his help.

Gingrich came up with the "Contract with America," and it gave the Republicans a national platform for a midterm election—something we had never seen before. It told the voters what they wanted to hear, and it had special appeal to this group that has become known as "angry white males." The result of all this was a smashing Republican victory.

After 1992, everybody wanted the 19 percent who voted for Ross Perot. In this midterm, 60 percent of those voters voted Republican. In this election it was Clinton and the Democrats who were painted as extreme, out of bounds, incompetent, and unable to govern. And so, the Republicans took over Congress, and it was a new experience for them and for us in the media. Bob Dole became majority leader and Newt Gingrich Speaker of the House.

Mark Shields had the best analysis that I have heard. He said, "The Republicans were playing good cop and bad cop, and the scary thing is that Bob Dole is the good cop."

For the Republicans it's only been half a victory. What they really want is to get the White House in 1996, and everything that happens in Congress has to be put in the context of a presidential campaign now.

Bill Kristol's slogan is "'96 or Bust." They have a plan, and they're going to use congressional power to set up a '96 presidential victory.

The House Republicans made good on their promise to pass the Contract with America. They didn't get it all, but they got almost everything. What counts now is the next two hundred days, or the rest of this year. The Senate is in no hurry and has real doubts about some of the key elements in this truckload of legislation. I asked one senior Republican, "You know the Senate's not going to pass all this stuff." And his reply was "Thank God for the Senate."

The real test of the Contract with America is going to be at the end of 1995, when we see how much has passed, how much was agreed on in the conference committees between the House and the Senate. What does the president sign or veto? And what lives or dies after a veto?

In the short term I think everyone likes the idea of a tax cut, and the bigger it is the better they like it. In the long term Americans may not like it if they find out that they got a tax cut, but their kids who were depending on college loans cannot get them because the funds been eliminated or greatly reduced. State and local government is very nervous about this program and the impact it will have on them.

I think it also depends, to a great extent, on how well the Democrats do in selling their party line—that the Republicans are helping the rich at the expense of the poor. It worked in previous campaigns when it was known as the "fairness issue," and I think it is something the Republicans have to worry about.

Just remember the words of Morris Udall, which I live by: "I've told you what I believe in, where I stand, what my principles are; and if any of you disagree I'll change my mind."

Budget Policy Under United Government: A Case Study

Robert D. Reischauer

ooking back over the first two years of the Clinton administration, it is clear that the administration's budget policy was very successful. Paradoxically, the administration has not received a political dividend for its success; instead, it has paid a fairly hefty price. This is not surprising, for when it comes to deficit reduction, no good deed goes unpunished, as George "Read my Lips" Bush can attest.

My presentation will review budget policy over the past two years—which is really just the story of 1993—to see what it tells us about effective governance when one party controls the House of Representatives, the Senate, and the White House—that is, when there is united government. To cut to the bottom line, I think there is one simple lesson that can be drawn from the recent experience. That lesson is that while united government may create the conditions under which budgetary gridlock can be overcome, it also can be politically destructive to the governing party. As such, it is destabilizing.

These consequences arise because the overriding objective of budget policy in recent years is deficit reduction, and that objective can be achieved only by inflicting pain and sacrifice. No rational individual, particularly one whose employment depends on currying favor with the electorate, should want such a responsibility. But united government forces this job onto one party, and in doing so it lets the other party off the hook. As a result, the budget policies pursued by the governing party are likely to be more extreme and subject to criticism than those that would be crafted in an environment of divided government, where both parties have to agree to the solution. Under united govern-

ment, however, the deficit reduction policies will be designed to maximize the votes of the members of the governing party alone rather
being reflective of the views of the median legislator. In addition, the
need for the president and the legislative leaders to impose discipline
may unleash forces that undermine the governing party's ability to
marshal its troops on other issues later on.

Let me start the story by laying out the three ingredients that had to
be mixed together in January 1993 when the Clinton administration
began to formulate its budget policy. The first of these was the activist
agenda that the new president had articulated in his campaign speeches
and in his book *Putting People First.* Candidate Clinton promised a
middle-income tax cut, some form of national service, policies to
rebuild the nation's public infrastructure, lifetime learning, welfare
reform, health reform, education and training programs to help narrow
the earnings gap, an expanded earned income tax credit (EITC), and so
on. No matter what the claims were, there was nothing thing cheap on
this list.

The second ingredient was the deteriorating budget outlook. When
the deficit agreement was approved in the fall of 1990, the
Congressional Budget Office (CBO) had estimated that the policies
included in that package would come close to balancing the budget by
1995. In other words, no heavy lifting would be required from the next
president. The 1990–91 recession, the failure to deal with the savings
and loan fiasco expeditiously, the rapacious manner in which states
went at the medicaid program through provider tax and donation
schemes, and dozens of other technical and economic developments
turned these projections into a fairy tale. In mid-1992 and early 1993,
CBO and the Office of Management and Budget boosted their deficit
projections significantly, signaling that further action would be
required if the new administration hoped to keep the deficit much
below $300 billion.

The third ingredient, of course, was the 1990 budget agreement,
which severely constrained the budgets for fiscal years 1991 through
1995. Under the procedural innovations that were part of this agreement, any changes in tax policy or entitlement programs had to be paid
for on a year-by-year basis under the pay-as-you-go (or paygo) require-
ments of the Budget Enforcement Act. In addition, total discretionary
spending was capped for the new administration's first two budgets
(fiscal years 1994 and 1995) at levels that required a slight reduction

in real or inflation-adjusted spending. One bit of wiggle room was given the new administration. The fire walls that dictated the division of discretionary resources between defense, international, and domestic uses for fiscal years 1991, 1992, and 1993 ended. The new president, therefore, had some freedom to shift resources from defense to domestic programs when he put together his fiscal year 1994 budget.

The new administration's budget policy, which the president unveiled in his February 17, 1993, speech to Congress, was a complex proposal.[1] It had three objectives: to stimulate the sluggish economy in the short run, to reorient tax and discretionary spending policy to encourage long-run economic growth and help vulnerable populations,[2] and to make a major contribution to long-run deficit reduction through tax increases (primarily on upper-income groups) and spending cuts (primarily in entitlements).

The three objectives of the president's budget plan were in conflict. The stimulus initiative would make the deficit problem worse, and the reorientation of priorities meant that there had to be far more in the way of spending cuts and tax increases than would ever show up on the bottom line as deficit reduction. In fact, roughly 45 percent of the spending cuts and tax increases proposed by the president were needed just to pay for his proposed reorientation of priorities.

A traditional appraisal of the president's proposal might have predicted that it would be popular, particularly with Democratic constituencies, because it contained something for everyone and represented a sharp contrast with the policies of the Bush administration, which had seemed unengaged on all three fronts. But in a constrained world where every program expansion has to be paid for before the deficit reduction game can even begin, providing something for everyone implies that something has to be taken away from many as well. Understandably, most constituencies value a bird in the hand more than two in the bush.

Although the president's proposal might have received an A-plus in a budget policy seminar at the Kennedy School of Government, Congress proved to be a tougher grader. After the initial obligatory outpouring of partisan euphoria, considerable opposition developed within the Democratic ranks in Congress.

One reason for this was the unified opposition of the Republicans, which placed the Democrats on the defensive. The election had freed the Republicans from any need to be responsible or to govern. They therefore had little reason to support proposals that would inflict pain on their constituents. The fact that Republicans agreed strongly with two of the president's three goals—deficit reduction and resource reorientation to stimulate long-term growth—did not mean they had to be supportive. They could disagree with the president's means of achieving these objectives, which they did enthusiastically.

Republicans took great pleasure in criticizing the aspects of the president's plan that were most likely to affect Democratic constituencies—the BTU tax, the increased tax on social security benefits, the medicare cuts, and so on. They also reveled in the discovery that the tax increases and spending hikes associated with the stimulus package and the reorientation of priorities made the plan vulnerable to the dreaded tax-and-spend charge. This charge was credible because the proposed spending increases in the president's plan exceeded the proposed spending cuts for fiscal years 1993, 1994, and 1995, and there were net tax increases in all five years.

A second reason for the discomfort among the Democrats was the confusion and complexity caused by the contradictory nature of the proposal's three elements. The message was garbled.[3] Many Democrats (especially those from areas of the country that were not still hurting from the recession) saw little need for the stimulus package if it was going to raise the deficit in the short term. Others objected to the reorientation of priorities. They saw cuts in programs affecting their regions—grazing and hard rock mining fees, for example—being used to pay for expanded assistance to low-income people or programs whose benefits were concentrated in other regions of the country. Some were not enthusiastic about the stimulus package, because the spending measures it contained looked a lot like a grab bag of pork projects designed to please traditional liberal Democratic constituencies.

A third source of opposition was procedural in nature. Some important and many not-so-important Congressional players felt that they had not been consulted sufficiently in the formulation of the president's plan. There had been twelve years without a Democrat in the White House, and Congressional Democrats had become accustomed to calling the tune. Now they smarted at being asked to rubber stamp a presidential proposal that they had played little part in developing. They believed that the proposal contained some policy mistakes and political misjudgments that could have been avoided if the president had consulted more with Congress. For example, the members could have told the president that the stimulus package would never fly when deep spending cuts and tax increases were also being proposed. If consulted, they also could have told the president that the spending in his budget for fiscal year 1994 had to conform to the caps set by the budget resolution rather than those in the Budget Enforcement Act. This led to considerable embarrassment and heartburn when the president proposed some $12 billion in budget authority and $5.7 billion in outlays more than was allowed by the resolution's caps.

This last issue raises an interesting question—namely, for united government to work, do the executive branch and the congressional majority have to work closely together, and on a more equal footing, on the formulation of major policy initiatives?[4] Sharing this responsibility, of course, goes against every instinct of the executive branch; this is particularly true when a new administration is trying to establish an identity and to assert its dominant role as the agenda-setter.

The conditions that faced the Clinton administration were far from normal. For one thing, much of the Democratic party's policy formulation expertise had gravitated to Capitol Hill during the twelve-year period when the Republicans controlled the executive branch. In many ways, the congressional staff had more ability to put together the budget proposals than did the new political appointees, who were still trying to figure out how the White House phone system worked or where the Labor Department's cafeteria was located.

Second, the president was not of Washington but from a small state; therefore, his political judgement on national policy issues could be more easily questioned by the old hands on Capitol Hill.

Third, with 43 percent of the popular vote in the election, the president was hardly a political force that commanded the attention and loyalty of his congressional troops. Virtually all of the congressional Democrats had captured a higher percentage of the votes in their district than the president had.

Although some in Congress may have hoped that there would be meaningful and extensive consultation and collaboration on budget matters now that united government had returned, one wonders whether that was or ever could be a realistic expectation. For one thing, consultation takes time, and where the budget is concerned there is not much leeway. The budget resolution, reconciliation legislation, and appropriation bills had to be in place by the start of the fiscal year in October.

In this respect, the Clinton administration found itself in a particularly difficult position, because the outgoing Bush administration had not prepared a serious budget proposal embodying policy prescriptions. Instead it had left behind a current policy or baseline sketch of what would happen if policies were not changed. Unlike other new administrations, the Clinton team therefore had to formulate an entire budget and could not just propose a few dozen changes to an existing budget proposal. Consultation would have had to range across a broad array of areas and would have been unmanageable.

Another consideration is that parties in Congress, particularly the Democrats, are not monolithic blocks when it comes to policy views. Nor are they groups with single hierarchical leadership structures. On any issue, there are several powerful players in the leadership and who chair important committees and subcommittees. Each has a separate power base and a different view of the problem and its appropriate solution. Each is likely to consider him- or herself the essential contact for the executive branch. None can be offended, because each may be able to stop the administration's proposal from moving forward. However, none of these individuals has the authority, power, or troops needed to ensure that if he or she is satisfied with the president's plan, it will move forward in both chambers. Senator Robert Byrd's assurances to the president on the stimulus package and Chairman John Dingell's promises on health care reform underscore this fact.

In short, consultation could lead to confusion rather than coherence, to disunity rather than unity. It could produce raised expectations and greater frustration among those whose views were not included in the administration's final legislative proposal. For example, conservative Democrats might have been even more upset if the president had insisted on using reductions in the defense budget to fund his domestic initiatives after he had consulted with them and they had urged him to boost defense spending.

Let me return to the story.

United government clearly allowed the budget resolution for fiscal year 1994 to sail easily and expeditiously through the budget committees and the votes on the House and Senate floors. For the first time in the history of the budget process, the resolution was approved before the Budget Act's April 15 deadline.[5]

One reason why the resolution had such smooth sailing had to do with the nature of budget resolutions: Nothing in them except the aggregate spending and revenue numbers and the committee totals for the reconciliation instructions is binding. Resolutions lack the specificity of budgets or appropriation and reconciliation bills. Although the resolution did conform to the plan that the president laid out on February 17, the administration's detailed budget proposal was not released until a week after the resolution was approved. Therefore, the contentious detail was not available and tough issues could be finessed.

A second important reason for smooth sailing, of course, was the Democrats' realization that they had to deliver now that they controlled both the legislative and executive branches of government. After years of budgetary conflict and gridlock with Republican presidents, Democrats had to show they could bite the deficit reduction bullet by themselves. This made the liberal Democratic leadership willing to accommodate the conservative wing of the party as soon as it became clear that there would be no moderate Republican votes for the resolution. The specter of the Democratic defections that occurred in 1981 ensuring passage of the Reagan tax and budget plans haunted them.

The leaders agreed to let the stimulus initiative (which they favored) wither in the Senate. They also went along with a budget resolution that incorporated more spending cuts, more deficit reduction, and fewer tax increases than the president had proposed.

For their part, the conservatives and other hesitant Democrats were willing to overlook some of the specific policy proposals they found objectionable, arguing that the budget resolution did not lock in the specifics; these would be decided in the reconciliation and appropriation bills. In the Senate, the leaders held the Democratic coalition together by providing a number of sense of the Senate resolutions—on taxes, social security, defense spending, levies on home heating oil and agricultural uses, the line item veto, and hard rock mining and grazing fees—which were designed to provide political cover to wavering Democrats.

Of course, the real budget battle developed over the reconciliation bill that was to set budget policy for the next five years. Here the specifics couldn't be ignored. This legislation contained the language that raised taxes, cut entitlement spending, increased the EITC and food stamps, established empowerment zones, set new discretionary spending caps, and so on. Despite comfortable majorities in both houses of Congress, intense pressure from the leadership, and direct retail lobbying by the president, the vice president, and members of the cabinet, the reconciliation bill passed with no votes to spare and no support from the Republicans.

The House version of the reconciliation bill passed 219 to 213, with 10 Democratic subcommittee chairmen voting against it. In the Senate, Vice President Gore's vote was needed to break a 49 to 49 tie. When the conference report was voted on in the House, the vote was 218 to 216, with Marjorie Margolies-Mezvinsky casting the vote that not only decided the bill's fate but also that of her congressional career. In the Senate, the vice president once again was called on to decide the issue in a 51 to 50 vote. Joining the opposition were six Democrats— Chairmen Nunn and Johnston, Subcommittee Chairmen Bryan and Lautenberg, and Senators Shelby and Boren.

The final reconciliation bill was fashioned solely to maximize Democratic votes because there was no reason, under unified government, for Republicans to associate themselves with the unpopular specifics of deficit reduction. Although the original presidential proposal was pushed to the right to keep conservative Democrats from bolting, the movement was nowhere near as much as would have been the case had there been the shared responsibility of divided government under which some Republican participation would have been required. The package therefore remained firmly anchored on the left by threats of defection from the liberal wing of the Democratic party. As a result, it had a heavy emphasis on taxes—some 62 percent of the policy-related deficit reduction came from taxes. It is worth noting that the 1990 deficit reduction agreement, which was crafted by the Democratic leadership in a divided government environment, relied on tax increases for only 35 percent of its policy-related deficit reduction.[6] The tax increases in the 1993 package were very progressive— higher taxes on the rich, and generous EITC benefit expansions for low-income families.

Similarly, under the appropriation bills, the defense budget was to bear all of the burden of the discretionary spending cuts. In fact, domestic discretionary spending grew in real terms over the Clinton administration's first two years.

What are we to conclude from this experience? The president's budget policy was a success. He was able to put in place a major policy change relying solely on the support of his party. The policy achieved the objectives he had laid out. The deficits for 1994–98 have been reduced by the actions taken in 1993 by a cumulative total of $433 billion. The actual deficits have fallen from $290 billion in 1992, to $255 billion in 1993, to $203 billion in 1994, to a projected $161 billion in the current year. Although much of this decline is attributable to the economic recovery and technical factors, the president's policies have contributed importantly to the improved situation.

Priorities have been reoriented, although not as much as the president proposed. Defense spending has been cut well below the levels outlined by the Bush administration and spending on education, training, child nutrition, vulnerable populations, and science and technology has been increased.

Even though the stimulus package never was approved, the economy has grown strongly and has been operating at or a bit above full capacity for the better part of a year. Inflation remains relatively low, and there is every reason to expect the economy will experience a soft landing.

And yet the president and the Democratic party have not been credited with any accomplishment. Because of this, the success of united government in handling budget policy in 1993 was probably not replicable. Even if the Democrats had retained control of both Houses of Congress in the 1994 elections and even if the president had wanted to take another major step toward balancing the budget, it is unlikely that he could have mustered the needed support from his own party in Congress (let alone any from the Republicans) for a second effort.

The success he had in 1993 in many ways was attributable to the unwillingness congressional Democrats felt abouting blowing up the new administration just as it was trying to get off the launch pad. The administration was new; it was weak; the public's attention was focused on the votes, and members did not want to bring an administration of their party to its knees so soon. This view was best expressed by Senator Bob Kerrey, who sent his message to the president through the TV cameras after emerging from an afternoon in a movie theater. Kerrey had been contemplating his vote on the reconciliation bill and said to the president, "I could not and should not cast the vote that brings down your presidency."

But the experience left a bitter taste in the mouths of many Democrats, and they have no desire to go through it again. They realize now, as they had suspected in 1993, that there is no political payoff or reward to effective governance when the task of governing means inflicting pain and imposing restraints.

So the budget policy represents a case study of an event that probably can occur only once during each episode of unified government. When it succeeds, it boosts the political fortunes of the opposition and begins to fragment the unity of the governing party.

The 1993 budget package may be viewed by historians as one of the bright spots of the Clinton administration. But for the good of the political system and for the most enlightened deficit reduction policies, budget policy in an environment of fiscal retrenchment is probably done best when it occurs during a period of divided government. If both parties are forced to participate, the responsibility for inflicting pain must be shared, and the specific measures used to cut spending and raise taxes are more likely to reflect the middle of the political spectrum.

Consciously or unconsciously, the new Republican leadership in Congress seems to understand this. That is why it wants to enact policies to balance the budget now, when a Democrat is in the White House and can share in the blame. If the Republicans can move forward this year and get the president involved, whatever is enacted will be better for the nation and better for both political parties in the long run. The alternative is to have the Republicans hold the knife alone in 1997. If they do so, they will be punished—just as the Democrats were punished when they held the knife alone in 1993.

Notes

1. The Clinton administration's detailed revised 1994 budget was not released until April 8.

2. Along these lines, more resources were provided for AIDS, the EITC, housing, child nutrition, and Head Start.

3. This is not unlike the situation the Republicans faced in the spring of 1995 as they attempted to justify deep tax cuts as part of their package to balance the budget by 2002.

4. This same question could be raised with respect to health care reform.

5. The budget resolution was approved on April 1, 1993.

6. The 1990 package is usually described as the product of the Budget Summit, but this is wrong. The Summit proposal was defeated in the House, and the Democratic leadership fashioned the ultimate package.

Health Care Reform: A Case Study

Robin Toner

It seems hard to believe from the perspective of 1995 that once upon a time the passage of major health care legislation seemed absolutely inevitable. Nobody in Washington much likes to admit they ever believed this, just as nobody much likes to admit that back in the spring of 1991 the reelection of President Bush seemed inevitable. But this was in fact the conventional wisdom, and in the spirit of full disclosure, I will acknowledge that I shared it.

In the spring of 1993 all of the prerequisites seemed to be in place for the creation of a vast new domestic program. There was a growing consensus among policy elites and the business community that something had to be done about rising health costs. There was a stack of polls showing that the public overwhelmingly (by 80 or 85 percent) believed there was in fact a health care crisis and that the system needed to be fundamentally rebuilt.

Perhaps most important of all, there was a newly elected Democratic president who had explicitly campaigned on this issue and badly wanted to deliver on it. He was joined by Democratic leaders on Capitol Hill who had spent much of their adult lives waiting for an opportunity just such as this: a great social need, a Democrat in the White House, a chance to exercise all the possibilities of an activist government.

Democrats had been battle tested on the budget. In short, there was every indication that Democrats recognized their common interest in doing something big and something right on health care. They recognized that this was perhaps a unique opportunity to cement the voters' loyalties after twelve long years of being shut out of the White House.

There are a lot of explanations for what turned the great health care drive of 1993 into the legislative train wreck of 1994. Journalists like myself spent a lot of time last fall picking through the wreckage. Perhaps predictably for my profession, we spent a lot of time talking about strategic and tactical errors—errors that had to do with process.

For example, some have argued that the Clinton administration simply created a bad process with its closed-door, strangely mysterious task force under Hillary Rodham Clinton and Ira Magaziner, a task force that was cut off from the normal political loop on Capitol Hill and almost inevitably produced a politically tone-deaf plan.

It is argued that President Clinton himself simply made a series of strategic miscalculations—that he should have pushed for less, or he should have pushed for passage of the bill in 1993, or he should have pushed earlier for a bipartisan deal in 1994.

But there were so many underlying big reasons for the failure that it is hard to know whether even the most brilliant tactician or strategist in the White House could have succeeded in this time frame, particularly a president elected with only 43 percent of the vote and contending with the ideological divisions that characterize politics on this issue today.

I will offer a few thoughts on some of the deeper causes that I think explain why a party with so much at stake on an issue was nevertheless unable to deliver. Some of these causes had to do with the party; some of them have to do more generally with the way we practice politics today.

Let me begin with the party. There is real irony in the way the years 1993–94 are referred to as a period of united government (as distinct from the twelve years of divided government from 1981 through 1992), because Democrats were not in a fundamental way united. Real unresolved ideological tensions in the party were masked by the victory in 1992, and the health care issue brought them all to the forefront. There were tensions around peripheral issues, as would exist in any party, but also around fundamentals—namely, what is the proper role of government in attempting to achieve a vast social good, affordable health care for every American?

President Clinton, a child of the conservative or centrist Democratic Leadership Council, clearly thought that he had transcended or bridged these tensions during the campaign. He ran as the candidate of the third way, promising a government that was neither of the left nor the right, neither passive nor intrusive, but a focused and activist agent for the betterment of the forgotten middle class.

As it turned out though, the third way was a lot easier to chart in rhetoric than it was in real-life policy. The ideological tensions, I think, explain in part why the Clinton administration's health care plan was so immensely complex. So much of that famous organizational chart Senator Dole took such pleasure in distributing, with its web of regional health alliances and its complicated redistribution of premiums, can be seen as an attempt to find that elusive third way. It was an attempt to provide health insurance to every American—obviously a long-time goal of the left—while avoiding the appearance of direct government involvement in financing and running the health care system, which was a major concern of conservative Democrats.

I remember having fierce discussions with Clinton administration officials over whether the alliances were in fact a vast new layer of government. Others will recall fierce arguments over whether the mandated premiums that were going to be imposed on employers were in fact a tax.

Of course, despite all of the administration's efforts to explain the health care industry, the Republican party succeeded in portraying the Clinton plan as a government takeover of one-seventh of the American economy.

When the struggle over health care moved to Capitol Hill, these unresolved tensions could be seen in the development of some distinct, dug-in Democratic camps. On the left were the single-payer supporters in the House, about 80 or 90 liberal Democrats who believed in a Canadian-style system of national health insurance. At the other end of the continuum were conservative Democrats (many of them from the South) who supported only the most modest, incremental reforms. In between there were the managed competition purists like Representative Jim Cooper, who believed that the Clinton plan had been pushed too far to the left, reflected way too much government, and had betrayed the central tenets of managed competition. And scattered around the middle was an array of other factions worried about the impact on rural areas, or urban areas, or big hospitals, or (most particularly) small employers.

One question obviously arises: isn't this where party leadership comes in? If health care legislation was so important to the Democrats, as the 1994 election suggested, couldn't some consensus be forged by party leadership once the plan got to Capitol Hill? After all, House Republicans were hardly unanimous on every element of the Contract with America. Nevertheless, they managed to pass most of it, at least in the first round.

But the Democratic majority in the House then was run very differently from today's new Republican majority. Whereas Newt Gingrich as Speaker of the House has consolidated power in the party leadership and assured that committee chairmen owe their first loyalty to him, power was much more diffuse and divided under the Democrats. This is probably not surprising. The Democrats had been in power for forty years. A variety of independent and often competing power bases had developed on the committees, with chairmen like Dan Rostenkowski on Ways and Means and John Dingell on Energy and Commerce, who had watched presidents (not to mention Speakers of the House and majority leaders) come and go. The strength of the committees in the House meant that five of them had jurisdiction over health care. It was a remarkably Byzantine process that could not have been better designed to sap the health care drive of its political and public opinion momentum.

The Democrats in the House were also slowed down by a legacy of the budget battle: their suspicions of the Democrats in the Senate. Many of the Democrats in the House thought they had walked the plank on the btu tax, only to see it jettisoned by the Senate. A common refrain among House Democrats in the spring of 1994 was that they were not going to be "BTU-ed" again. A case can be made, of course, that even if the Democratic House had managed to act on health care reform, the bill would have faced real problems in the Senate. But the fact remains that the bill bogged down in a Democratic House in Democratic committees while a Democratic White House watched in dismay.

And time proved to be a real killer of health care. Here we need to look at factors that transcend the problems of the Democratic party, because this was not simply a struggle within or between two parties. The Democrats were not simply fighting the Republicans, and they were not simply fighting among themselves. Mining every division, every weakness, every wavering member on a committee was an extraordinary array of well-organized, well-financed interest groups willing to spend, poll, and advertise to protect their interests. Some make the argument that this is nothing new. During the debate over medicare in 1964, an immense amount of lobbying, leafleting, and mailing went

on—a normal feature of a major public policy debate in American politics. But I contend that it is something new: the application of all the
technology of the modern campaign to the policymaking process does
fundamentally change the nature of that process.

Consider Harry and Louise—the famous Harry and Louise—carefully tested in focus groups, produced by a seasoned political consul-
tant (who incidentally happens to consider himself a liberal), carefully
targeted to educated women who followed the issues and were likely to
communicate with Congress. Every group worth its salt was polling
consistently, while politicians were getting polls of their own, measuring the impact of the unfolding debate. As the months passed, and the
legislation languished in committee, and the advertising and lobbying
intensified, public opinion began to turn decisively against a major
health care overhaul. At that point the power of the toughest committee chairman to sway his members to cast hard votes (like a vote for an
employer mandate) was simply overwhelmed. The campaigns against
health care reform were remarkably savvy and targeted right at
America's long-standing ambivalence toward government. The desire
for secure and affordable health care gave way to the fear of a government takeover.

When I traveled out in the country during several congressional
recesses in 1993–94, I was struck by how dramatically public opinion
turned on this subject. It reached the point where members of Congress
were being told by angry elderly people that they wanted the government kept out of their health care system. These were people, of
course, who were covered by a thirty-year-old government program
known as medicare.

By the summer of 1994, when some grand compromise on health
care might have been expected, the debate was utterly polarized and
partisan, similar to the end stages of a particularly brutal, modern presidential campaign, like 1988. Democratic leaders on the Hill were desperately trying to distance themselves from the Clinton plan and
somehow get a fresh start, but there was simply no safe ground on
which bipartisan compromise could bloom.

As for the role and responsibility of the media, who have been criticized for emphasizing the "horse race" aspects of the health care
debate rather than educating the public, I can only speak for the *New
York Times*. We tried very hard not to get caught up excessively in the
horse race. Obviously it was an extraordinary legislative struggle and

we had to write about the conflict among all the interests that were coming to bear. Along the way, we also tried hard to explain the issues. But this was an immensely complicated subject that sometimes seemed to overwhelm not only the political system but also the press as we tried to explain to our readers what was at stake.

Most of us who cover politics and particularly the policymaking process watch the poll numbers. We see how people can be swayed, particularly policymakers and elected officials. We see a closed loop of people reacting and moving in one direction, and the elected officials reacting, and then people moving in another direction, and so on.

When I was covering health care, I often wondered what it would have been like if there had been this kind of polling in the 1930s when the Social Security Act was being passed. There was some polling, but nothing like what we have today. I could just see FDR being told, "Oh no, you can't go to a payroll tax. I mean, my God!"

So what are the lessons of all this?

It is really not an idle question. The Republicans are about to turn to a health care overhaul themselves, this time on medicare. Now they find themselves trying to make the case that there is indeed a crisis in the health care system, and attempting to lay the groundwork for major change. Interestingly, the Republicans are running into some of the same problems the Democrats faced on this issue.

One lesson might be that even in a united government, an issue with as much potential for controversy as health care can be dealt with only in a bipartisan setting. The issue cuts to the heart of American fears and attitudes about government, and it affects the interests of vast and powerful segments of the American economy—from doctors to hospitals and to the big insurance companies.

Is it possible to talk about the transformation of medicare to a managed care system in a bitterly partisan climate when so many Democrats remember how they were pilloried by the Republicans on these issues last year? It's so easy, politically, for Democrats to raise the alarm about a forced march of elderly Americans into health maintenance organizations (HMOs), in an effort to save money for tax cuts for the rich. The early signs for the Republicans in the way this debate is unfolding are inauspicious.

Another lesson might be that no matter which party is in power, or whether government is divided or united, there is a powerful new dynamic at work in this system that the Framers of the Constitution

never really envisioned. A case can be made that the deadlock on
health care is a monument not to the Framers' system but to what we
have done to it—a brutal example of what happens when the tools,
techniques, and philosophy of the modern political campaign are
brought to bear on the policymaking process.

I believe the eighteen-month-long struggle over health care did not
carry this country to a new consensus on the issue. Public opinion was
carefully measured and then whipsawed around competing fears of
government bureaucrats, rationing, or loss of a trusted doctor. In such
a climate—in the heat of the campaign, in other words—there seemed
to be little room for consensus building. For that matter, there was little room for leadership in the classic sense, which educates and
informs rather than simply responds to a set of contradictory and competing fears and wants.

These are all factors that transcend any tactical or strategic blun-
ders. These concerns should give the Republicans pause as they try to
figure out how to handle the great health care struggle to come.

Divided Government: The Republican Takeover of Congress (1995–96)

The Voters' Perspective

Becky Cain

The questions we are addressing in this book are going to be upper-most in our minds as we enter the 1996 election, when the voters will again face intense scrutiny by politicians, political consultants, pollsters, and pundits. The 1994 elections brought revolution to the House and government divided, once again, between the parties.

Now, after the opening weeks of the 104th Congress, everyone wants to know what that elusive, mysterious, yet all powerful entity, the American electorate, thinks about its new Congress.

We will not find the answer reading the polls, since they are telling us very little about the electorate. Polls show us what most Americans think. But in 1994, as in all midterm elections, most Americans did not vote. Six out of every ten citizens stayed home on election day last year.

So let us not confuse the voters' perspective with that of the people as a whole. When we talk about the voters' perspective, we need to distinguish which voters we mean. Are we speaking of the 76 million voters who voted in 1994, the 104 million who voted in 1992, or the 68 million who voted in 1990? After all, two-thirds of the current Senate was elected in 1990 and 1992. All three electorates together, not just the most recent one, created the current government and the divisions within that government.

The distinction is critical because the 1994 electorate looks very different from the 1992 electorate. In 1994, the electorate had fewer African Americans. In the 1992 presidential election, 11 percent of the electorate was black. This number dropped to 9 percent in 1994. In addition, among blacks who did vote, fewer voted Republican in 1994.

Also, fewer women turned out in 1994. In 1992 they made up 54 percent of the electorate, but in 1994, only 51 percent.

Three years ago the gender gap had a decisive impact on the election. There really was little change in the gender gap in 1994, but since turnout among women was down, women's votes only decided the outcome in a very few races.

The 1994 electorate had a higher percentage of men and was less racially diverse than the electorate that voted for President Clinton. The 1994 electorate was also smaller. Turnout was up slightly in 1994, but only one percentage point above the average for the last four midterm elections. The total number of voters was still small—very small; only 39.5 percent of the voting age population voted. Republicans won 50.5 percent of the national vote last year. That is not a landslide. On a district-by-district basis (and that is what counts in deciding control of the House), the election was incredibly close. If fewer than 20,000 voters had switched their votes in the thirteen closest elections, Democrats would have maintained control of the House. Turnout matters.

Republicans owe their victory in the House to the well-organized, well-funded interest groups that got the vote out. The Christian Coalition, the term limits movement, and the National Rifle Association did their jobs. You do not have to agree with their positions to appreciate how effective they were. These groups advertised the same message. They waged an us-against-them battle against the federal government. With few exceptions, their efforts were successful. They energized their constituencies and they turned out the vote.

The importance of turnout shows in one of the races the Democrats did win. Senator Charles Robb won in Virginia, defeating Oliver North. North made his opposition to the federal government the centerpiece of his campaign. This was a competitive, highly visible race in which both sides worked hard at the grassroots level to energize their constituents. Turnout was high—50 percent—and the electorate looked more like the 1992 electorate. With women concerned about choice and African American leaders working to turn out supporters for Robb, he won. Once again, turnout matters.

As the next election approaches, the political consultants will be analyzing what worked in 1994. They will find (indeed, they already know) that campaigning against government can be a highly effective tool. The campaign was like a great bellows, puffing away to fan the flames of suspicion, resentment, anger, and frustration. The voters, of course, had a right to be angry. The 103d Congress, under Democratic rule with no Republican president to blame, had failed to bring campaign finance reforms, or what the 1992 electorate had asked for: health care and welfare reform. This justifiable frustration was expertly exploited in subtle and not so subtle ways.

I know because I had the pleasure of being on several radio talk shows to discuss term limits, which was a hot-button campaign issue. I can tell you from personal experience that people are angry. Term limits focused that anger. Many supporters of and term limits earnestly believe that such limits offer a solution to the troubles they see in Congress. Some want term limits because they believe that the limits will make Congress more effective.

For campaign consultants, however, the term limits movement was nothing more than a brand-new, shiny tool to be used to elect their candidates—candidates with an antigovernment message.

As a result of these effective campaigns, Republicans were vaulted into the pilot's seat in Congress, opposing the Democratic president. Did the 1994 electorate deliberately vote for divided government? No.

Different electorates voting at different times led to our country's divided government. The 1994 divisions created another division as well. Not only is Congress divided from the executive branch, the House is divided from the Senate. The defeat of the House Balanced Budget Constitutional Amendment in the Senate underscores this division. In the first one hundred days the conflicts between the House and Senate over the line-item veto, regulatory reform, tax cuts, and welfare reform made this division strikingly apparent. The real revolution that occurred in the 1994 election was not a change in party; it was the change within the House, specifically the rise to power of the antigovernment wing of the GOP.

The new division cuts between those who believe that the federal government has a positive role to play and those who would cripple it. The legislative agenda of the new House can be traced directly to the groups who worked to energize the voters who gave the Republicans their victory.

On the first day of the 104th Congress, the House began working to undercut congressional power. After twenty minutes of debate, on the first day of the congressional session, the House passed a rules change requiring a so-called supermajority vote to pass any income tax rate increases. In the fervor of the takeover, this rules change was an infinitesimal blip on the national radar screen. And yet, if you look closely, you can see the agenda for the next one hundred days spelled out in that one deft legislative move.

House Rule XXI requires a three-fifths majority vote to raise taxes. This was the first of many feel-good, quick-fix solutions that would be offered in the House. This one happens to be unconstitutional. Why? Because it turns the principle of majority rule on its head, by handing over the most important power given to the House—the power to lay taxes—to the minority. This was constitutional change on the sly.

House Rule XXI is like planned obsolescence. Its purpose is to tie the hands of the legislature. Nearly all tax legislation will include a tax rate increase, even if overall taxes go down in the legislation. House Rule XXI enables all important tax legislation to be controlled by a minority vote. It is a model piece of antigovernment legislation. Like House Rule XXI, much of the House's legislative agenda has but one purpose: to undermine the role of the federal government. It is no accident that we saw two constitutional changes proposed—constitutional amendments for a balanced budget and for term limits. These amendments promised the people more than a slight policy shift; they promised a radical power shift.

Indeed, it is hard to find a piece of House legislation that does not shift power away from Congress. Block grants and the unfunded mandates legislation transfer power to the states. Term limits and the line-item veto transfer power to the executive branch. Regulatory reform transfers power to corporations to regulate themselves. The balanced budget amendment, as passed in the House, would have transferred power to the courts. In working to legislate this antigovernment agenda, the House was responding to the desires of the electorate that had cast the deciding ballots and the groups who had worked hard for GOP victory. The speed and finesse with which this legislation was pushed through the House shows, however, that strong leadership can make the political process work.

Now approval ratings for Congress have gone up, even though the majority of Americans have disapproved of the content of the legislation. This paradox is no mystery. The public wants effective government. President Clinton, after all, won election with a campaign that promised positive, effective government.

What will the future hold? Will divided government continue after

1996, or will Congress and the President be held by the same political party? Most important, will Congress and the presidency be held by officials who share a common outlook and philosophy of government?

To answer these questions, we need to look a little closer at the 1996 electorate. We can be sure of one thing: in 1996, we are going to have a wholly new electorate. It is going to be much larger, more diverse, and more reflective of the population. Because of the National Voter Registration Act (NVRA, known as the "motor voter" law), the electorate in 1996 will be substantially different.

"Motor voter" went into effect in January 1995. The new law requires that states offer citizens voter registration opportunities when they apply for a driver's license, for public assistance, or for disability services. It also requires states to offer registration by mail. In the first month of operation, the states reported more than a half a million new voter registrants under the NVRA. This number dwarfs the number from the previous January. The reports for the first quarter of 1995 suggest that 2 million have now registered. Further, those percentages will increase dramatically when California, Pennsylvania, Illinois, and Michigan begin to implement the law.

Some have estimated that we will have 20 million new voters by 1996. In 1996, as before, turnout will make the difference. Voters make the fundamental decisions. The composition of the electorate—who votes, who is energized to vote, who is motivated to vote—will determine the outcome.

The Capitol Hill Perspective: A Democratic View

Thomas J. Downey

One of my closest friends in the House of Representatives is Congressman Jim McDermott, whose prior occupation was as a child psychiatrist. As a result, he has a unique insight into the House of Representatives and its members. He was actually quoted in the papers early in 1995 when somebody asked, "What's happening in the House caucus?" And he said, "Well, you know there are four stages that individuals go through when they are diagnosed with a disease like cancer. The first is shock, the next is anger, then there is denial, and then finally acceptance." He said basically the caucus was in four stages: some were shocked; some were angry; some were in denial; and some had accepted the fact that, for the first time in forty years, people who had come to the House of Representatives to govern and play a role in writing legislation and micromanaging the federal government were now not in a position to do that.

Indeed, the Democratic caucus was very deeply divided over a lot of issues. And in fact, even though there are 201 nominal Democrats, the reality is that in the House of Representatives there are really only about 170 Democrats that could be counted on to vote for some national Democratic agenda. There are about thirty fairly conservative Democrats who will routinely vote with Republicans—and did so on House changes and on a number of elements in the Contract with America.

So the Democrats have been in the process of finding their voice and articulating an agenda. And probably the most important thing for them to understand—and it is a painful one, and probably shocking to

44

some—is that they need to resist the temptation to govern because they are not in charge anymore. And the House rules amply demonstrate that a strongly motivated, wisely led, and disciplined group can have its way in the House of Representatives.

What happened with the Contract with America was truly extraordinary. No other Speaker of the House in this century, in my opinion, has had the direction, the ambition, and the power that the current Speaker has. Democrats must understand that if they are to have an impact and return to majority status, they need to focus their message, attention, energy, and the little money that they may have on the few issues that really matter to them, so that they can compare and contrast themselves with the Republicans. They have started to do that with issues like school lunches and education.

Next, Democrats will need to define where they are on the issue of health care. They have been aided in this effort by the Republicans' desire to take on some of the tough issues of the waning years of the twentieth century and actually try to devise a plan to balance the budget and to reform health care.

People who are really worried about gridlock need to understand one fundamental difference that has been brought home in these last several months by the Republicans. And that is that Democrats and Republicans disagree, and disagree quite fundamentally, about the role and the nature of government. In particular, the Democrats believe—not just because they are retrograde, or legatees of the work of Franklin Roosevelt and Harry Truman and John F. Kennedy and Lyndon Johnson and Jimmy Carter—that government has a place in the lives of individual Americans.

When they look at citizens, Democrats believe that they see something more than just taxpayers. They believe that yes, there should be individual initiative. But they also believe that there needs to be collective and community action—that government provides important responsibilities and the opportunity to make the lives of all Americans better, and that the national government (as opposed to the state government) is particularly important in dealing with national issues. Democrats look at the country and do not see a collection of fifty states—they see a nation.

And so, in term of contrasting themselves, Democrats for the most part do not want to turn welfare back to the states. In fact, welfare and income maintenance programs originally resided in the states. The reason over the last sixty years that the national government has taken over more and more of the responsibility is because we understand that the national government is the only place to provide a counter-cyclical effort to different states that are in poverty. Indeed, a lot of these problems are not unique to states but are unique to the country, and a national government needs to deal with these problems.

Republicans see the world differently. They want to replace national bureaucrats with state bureaucrats. They also want to do a whole host of other things that are in keeping with some of the finest traditions of the latest focus group and polling data. And to their credit, they have articulated an agenda and have stuck to it.

In the analysis of voters in the last election done by Curtis Gans, 5 percent of the people were actually out there voting for the Contract with America, and another 6 percent were out there voting against it. My former colleagues tell me that for the most part, the voters are very confused about what the Contract actually stands for.

So Democrats now have an opportunity during the remainder of the 104th Congress to try to define what the Contract with America means—to try to pose alternatives and to stop some of the worst elements of it. They are more likely, predictably, to succeed in the Senate than they are in the House, and that is what they should be about. If that means that there is more gridlock, more opposition, more partisan bickering, more consternation, more wringing of hands and gnashing of teeth in the American electorate about the fact that the Congress can't agree, then that is terrific. Congress cannot agree because it does not agree, and it should not.

Perhaps that is a lost message for some. But I noticed when I did town meetings, and I think my colleagues in the House are finding when they do theirs, that people are confused. If you make a compelling message about the national scene, you can get voters to move one way. If someone else then makes an equally compelling case, as Newt Gingrich and others do, talking about just bureaucrats, the voters can be moved the other way. The Republicans are wonderful at that. They never refer to people who work for the government by any other term, so that the process of demonization can be quite complete and thorough. Democrats in the House and Democrats in the Senate are going to have to take that head-on.

How they work with the president is another interesting question. Democrats like to embrace the president when he is popular and like to be independent of him when he is not. And we can expect that to continue. When the president's popularity continues to go up, more Democrats will be saying, "You know, this president is not so bad."

In the spring of 1995 there was some consternation with the president on two particular issues. The president rejected an appeal by 156 House Democrats to veto a tax bill, and he gave indications that he would sign a rescission package that Democrats are opposed to. Expect that bickering to continue. The Democrats in the House and the Senate have a role very different from the president's. They have to be the attack dogs, the pit bulls, in taking on the Contract with America. The president needs to step back from that and say that he can work with the Republicans on some issues and will oppose them on others. So their tasks are decidedly different.

But don't expect Dick Gephardt and Newt Gingrich to walk out into the Ellipse one day or in front of the Capitol with the dome silhouetted in the background and say, "We figured out what we need to do on health care. We have found the magic bullet for the balanced budget. We intend to operate harmoniously and in the spirit of the Founding Fathers to govern this country." That is not going to happen, and it should not happen. But what citizens should expect, and indeed require, from the Democrats is not just a lot of carping but, on occasion, a recitation of what it is we would do differently—and how it is we would do it.

If the Democrats decide simply to oppose without some underlying reason, we could be in even bigger trouble in 1996 than we were in 1994.

The Capitol Hill Perspective: A Republican View

Vin Weber

A couple of structural problems that have led to what we call grid-lock and that can be addressed. But they are only about 5 percent, maybe 10 percent, of the problem.

One of these problems—and one that is being dealt with—is weakened leadership particularly in the House of Representatives. The Speakers of the House that I served with were progressively weaker because of the proliferation of power within Congress. You remember Huey Long saying, "Every man a king." Now it's "every man a Speaker," or at least "every man a chairman." That weakened Speaker O'Neill, it weakened Speaker Wright, it weakened Speaker Foley as power was dispersed throughout Congress.

Newt Gingrich has acted swiftly, skillfully, and effectively to remedy as much of that problem as anyone possibly could in a limited period of time. He consolidated a lot of power back into the Speaker's office that had been lost (and some that was not there in the first place), and he has done about as much as can be done to override the power and prerogatives of the committee chairmen and try to herd them into a unified force. That's good. And it is one of the reasons the Contract with America was successful in coming out of the House, by and large, in the first one hundred days. That consolidation of power is going to help Gingrich to be effective in the remainder of this Congress.

However, a Speaker's strength is not entirely a question of his formal powers. An additional advantage for Gingrich is that this House Republican conference, perhaps uniquely in modern history, credits the Speaker with their being in the majority. That certainly is true of the freshmen members, but probably true more broadly as well. Whether it is entirely or only partially deserved is almost irrelevant. Most members think that without Newt Gingrich they would still be in the minority. So they are willing to cede to him a great deal of political moral authority to reinforce the structural changes that consolidate power in the Speaker's office.

The second major problem that has weakened our ability to organize public opinion and move agendas through Congress is something that is not getting any better, and that is weakened parties. Many people around this town such as David Broder have written about that, so I am not saying anything new. But I think it bears repeating, because it has not changed. And as the Congress grinds on and the issues become more contentious, it is likely that simply amassing power in the Speaker's office is not going to be sufficient in every case to override the other trend—this long-term decline in the strength of political parties.

That is a central issue facing us. Whenever you hear a story about the rising power of special interest groups, you ought to put in its place the declining power of political parties. We have always had special interest groups; they have a constitutional right to exist. The difference was that in the past we had political parties that filtered their claims on the government and organized popular opinion and political power to come to some sort of compromise on those conflicting claims and produce a governing agenda.

That does not happen anymore, because we have reformed the political parties into obsolescence. In my last year in Congress, when I was a member of the Republican Task Force on Campaign Finance Reform, Guy Vander Jagt and I came into this group of thirty Republicans one day with what we thought was a fairly noncontroversial motherhood-and-apple pie proposal. It was that whatever else we said about campaign finance reform, whatever positions we took on public financing and PACs and individual contribution limits, we should raise the party contribution limits because we are all in agreement that we want to strengthen parties. And at the end of a contentious discussion the number of advocates of that position numbered precisely two—Vander Jagt and me.

We found out that all of our colleagues (and I think this is probably true on the Democratic side as well) had deluded themselves into thinking that the last thing in the world they wanted was more accountability to their party chairmen back in their districts. They didn't seem to be terribly concerned about the fact that they had substituted an accountability to a wide array of special interest groups, some in their districts and some not.

But weakened parties have created the entrepreneurial class of congressional representatives as much as anything else. And they have weakened the claims of leadership, particularly when times get tough.

Those are the structural issues, and I think that they deserve some attention. But they are really secondary. The reason the Republicans and Democrats cannot agree is that Republicans and Democrats do not agree.

Maybe that is different today in some qualitative ways from what it used to be. People have been talking about a fundamental shift in our country's politics in the last few years. When he was in the White House, Jim Pinkerton talked about "the new paradigm." I think that he was saying something important, and his book is scheduled to come out in 1996 will develop it.

Professor Jim Reichley, right after this election, wrote that a realignment had occurred in different terms from those we traditionally have used—the first real intellectual and ideological realignment since the 1930s.

I tend to believe that. I think it explains the chaos that we have seen in the electorate, its uneasiness in recent years. We were thinking of electing Ross Perot because he was not a politician. Now the most popular politician in the country is Colin Powell, who is also not a politician. Seventy-five percent of the people say they have no use for either political party. New parties are making some progress around the country. The Republicans have a bit of an edge right now in terms of public confidence, but by and large people are still highly cynical and distrustful of government as a whole, which I think reflects a paradigm shift in the way people look at and think about government.

This is probably the first time that has happened since the New Deal. At that time the new people who had come into government with Roosevelt were committed to centralization, federal power, redistribution of income, standardization, and bureaucracy in the very best sense of the word—not in the sense that many of my Republicans friends use it to just beat up public employees who work hard and do a good job.

All of those notions were relatively new at that time. The European press thought it was the American manifestation of fascism.

Republicans here thought it was communism, or something like that, but it did not matter. People in FDR's administration were going about the business of reinventing government based on those principles, and it quickly became the wave of the future. And I would argue, as Reichley argues, that it has dominated our politics for the last sixty years. Eisenhower and Nixon were not exceptions to that. They may have changed the pace or the emphasis, but certainly Richard Nixon was controversial not because he helped establish the Occupational Safety and Health Administration and the Environmental Protection Agency and declared that we were all Keynesians, but rather because of the Vietnam War and Watergate.

Now we find that paradigm being rejected. The Republicans in office today do not share that view of the world, and that is tremendously important. Republicans and Democrats today are not just disagreeing on emphasis or on priorities. Republicans believe in state and local activity; Democrats believe in federal activity. Republicans believe in incentivizing people to produce, save, and invest, and Democrats believe in redistributing income. I am trying not to use loaded verbiage but to genuinely give some idea of the distinction between the parties. Both sides think they are right and virtuous.

These are fundamental disagreements that have to be worked out in the course of the next few years. On some issues, there may be bipartisan agreement consistent with this paradigm shift—perhaps, for example, on telecommunications deregulation—you certainly would not find any bipartisan agreement on reregulation—and possibly on welfare reform, provided the president is willing to sign a bill that moves in this direction.

The health care issue in the last Congress illustrated what is happening. At the end of the debate on health care, when we had interred the Clinton program, all of us around town said sagely that Clinton's health care proposal was doomed from the start because of—fill in the blank. Some said it was because he should have never put Mrs. Clinton in charge. Some said it was because Ira Magaziner fails at everything he tries. And others said other things.

I think the amazing thing about the Clinton health care proposal was that it did fail—that a Democrat President, having talked about a real problem, and not a made-up problem, came into office and tried to do something much in the way the Democrats have solved problems since the 1930s, and people were horrified by the end result of the process.

Some people say it was because of the media and the Republicans, and Newt Gingrich, and Rush Limbaugh, and G. Gordon Liddy. But the fact is the people rejected the plan because they learned it was bureaucratic, centralized, and costly. So what is new about that? Weren't the Great Society and the New Deal (to use loaded verbiage) centralized? Were they not bureaucratic? Were they not costly?

The amazing thing is that the country does not seem ready to accept this approach to problem solving anymore. Today, if you can successfully characterize a federal initiative to provide real benefits to middleclass people as being bureaucratic, costly, and centralized, public support for it will collapse—even though a president and a majority in both houses of Congress may be for it. That says a lot about our politics. That, more than anything else, produces the gridlock and the animus today. It will alleviate itself over time, but simple exhortation will not end the gridlock that seems to annoy all of us who are students of government. It is just not going to happen.

A White House Perspective

Kenneth M. Duberstein

Two years ago I was hopeful but far from optimistic that unified government would result in an end to gridlock. I was dubious for a variety of institutional reasons and political realities that one-party control of the Executive and Legislative Branches would make for "a get-things-done government." Today I am more hopeful but not sanguine that fundamentally gridlock can be broken in the aftermath of the 1994 election.

The voters on November 8 were saying to their elected leaders in Washington: "Stop the bickering, stop the fighting, stop the finger-pointing and get things done together in a commonsense way." They were repudiating Bill Clinton and his policies, especially the poster child of health care. Yet while the voters were signaling the end of forty years of Democratic control of the House, they were not giving a blank check to the Republicans to do anything that the new majority wanted.

They were saying to Bill Clinton: stop campaigning and govern. And they were saying the same thing to Newt Gingrich and Bob Dole.

During the first two years of the Clinton administration, in spite of one party control of both houses and the presidency, there was too much gridlock. There was still too much bickering, too many Clinton "landslide" votes of 218, too much, I think, governing from the left. The old Democratic bulls who controlled the House of Representatives did not want to jump to the new President's whip. And the public was confused by the presidential priorities. There were too many priorities and issues and therefore none became a priority. There was too little communication and even less repetition from the White House bully pulpit. One serious mistake was always to focus on getting 218 votes and not 250, or 260, or 270, because to get to 218, the last 10 votes became too expensive.

As surprised as many of us were last November, I do not think we should have been. The American people had elected to try one-party control and make the Democratic Party accountable, and guess what? It did not work. The deadlock on health care certainly was a key, in spite of the fact that the membership of the committees in the House of Representatives were heavily weighted toward accomplishing something on the Democratic side of the aisle.

So let me offer some snapshots.

Number one, the best parts of the first two years of the Clinton presidency were NAFTA, GATT, the conference report on the crime bill, and China's most favored nation status, because that is where a majority of each political party got together and did things in a common-sense way. It is where I think Bill Clinton was best at governing.

Second, Bill Clinton was absolutely magnanimous, he was wonderful in the aftermath of November 8, inviting down to the White House all the Democrats who had lost, for a series of meetings on lessons learned. I think his gesture was beautiful. But what troubled me was that he also should have invited down, if he really wanted to reach out and govern, all the Republicans who had won, for sessions on lessons learned, because that is how you reach out as a president and start building the roads to bipartisan victories later on.

Third, the Contract with America was a very good thing. It gave the Republican Party a strategy for governing in the initial months. It allowed Newt Gingrich and the Republican leadership in the House to override what any committee chairman wanted to do on his or her parochial agenda. It demonstrated from the Republican leadership an ability to say no to some in the party who were pushing other agendas. I think it was healthy because politicians—Republicans this time— actually were doing what they promised the American electorate. They were getting to vote on all the items of the Contract that were promised.

It is also interesting that, if I am not mistaken, an average of 47 Democrats supported each of the Contract items. They joined virtually a unanimous Republican Party in putting things together. It was not passing the Contract with 218, but with 250, 260, and in some cases 350 votes and pushing to 400.

Fourth, as somebody who feels he has been in Washington an awfully long time, I think this was the most active and the busiest first one hundred days of any Congress in my memory. After all, most Congresses in the initial one hundred days only organize their committees and subcommittees, and this time it was far different.

Fifth, the Senate will round the edges of a lot of what has come, and will come out of the House. That is somewhat healthy, and it is why we have a bicameral legislature. And Bob Dole and Newt Gingrich are working in relative harness. They know that governing well is the best public policy and politics, and stopping some of the gridlock in Congress helps each of them.

Sixth, I think the Democrats in Congress have a vested interest in gridlock. The only way, or at least probably the easiest way, for them to regain majority status is to deadlock Congress and the government. That is why I was quite taken in early 1995 with the spectacle of the Democrats going down to the White House and pleading with Bill Clinton to be more confrontational—to veto more, to argue more, to take a more vigorous stand from the bully pulpit. To put it in a different way, the congressional Democrats and the presidential Democrats do not necessarily have the same strategy or the same interests.

Seventh, President Clinton needs desperately to demonstrate an ability to govern, including not partisan but presidential, not willy-nilly vetoes but surgical vetoes. After all, as someone who had encouraged President Reagan to veto some bills, my view was always that a veto is an admission of failure that our system did not work. How can people be encouraged to work together? Perhaps by veto threats, but not actual vetoes. I was taken with President Clinton's remark in the State of the Union address, "I don't want a pile of vetoes," he said, "I want a pile of bills that will move this country into the future." I think he plays well when he plays Mr. Bipartisan, Mr. Outreach. The trouble is, in the first two years I think he did it too infrequently.

Fundamentally, the American people want to see a president who wants to govern, and to govern well President Clinton needs to be a full participant. He cannot just say no. When his trustees of medicare say that the Medicare Trust Fund is going to go bankrupt in seven years, or is going to be spending out more than it is taking in, he must propose something. He is going to have to start engaging in these discussions pretty soon.

Everyone focuses on the fact that this is the first time in forty years that the Republicans have controlled the House of Representatives. It's also the largest minority in Congress in forty years. It is not the mirror image of so many of the previous Congresses when there were 250 or 260 or 270 Democrats and 140, 150, 160, or 170 Republicans. The margin is very narrow. In my calculation there are between thirty and forty so-called moderate Republicans and about twenty-five or thirty conservative Democrats who hold the key to whether Newt Gingrich wins in the House or Bill Clinton has an opportunity to break through. And yet, President Clinton needs to start contesting those votes. He needs to start the outreach. It is not too late. The same is true in the Senate. The key there to breaking gridlock is eight to ten Republicans and eight to ten so-called moderate or conservative Democrats.

Newt Gingrich and Bob Dole understand the math quite well. That is why the moderate Republicans have stayed almost unanimously with Newt Gingrich on virtually all the Contract items. He has gone out and worked with them from day one, not at the eleventh hour. Similarly, Dole has tried to build alliances with some of the so-called moderate Senate Republicans.

Eighth, I have often argued, as I argued two years ago, that to be effective a president needs to be revered and feared, especially by the people on Capitol Hill. And yet to this day President Clinton is neither quite revered or feared. I think he has been a capable and strong leader on a few issues, but he needs to be viewed that way by many more on Capitol Hill (including members of the Democratic party) than he is today.

Finally, we have learned that unified government does not mean a get-things-done government. President Clinton should understand that if he is to be reelected, he must demonstrate an ability to govern, to make our institutions of government work together.

I think Speaker Gingrich understands that he is no longer a backbencher—that he must govern well if there are to be more Republicans in the next Congress. Majority Leader Dole understands that he too must govern well if he is to win the Republican nomination for the presidency and have a good shot at winning in November 1996, as well as to keep the Senate Republican.

Bill Clinton, Bob Dole, Newt Gingrich. None of them can afford the title Guardian of Gridlock. That is why I am hopeful today, certainly more hopeful than I was two years ago. But let us not be pollyannish. If gridlock remains, I think the American people will continue to channel surf, switching off each political party and each candidate until they get it right.

The Growing
Animus . . .

... Between the President and Congress

Howard H. Baker, Jr.

We have been paying a lot of attention over the last several months to the Republican capture of the House of Representatives and of the Senate in the elections just passed, and especially to the so-called Contract with America and the first one hundred days. We have been paying so much attention, in fact, that the president of the United States held a news conference not long ago to remind us that he was relevant to our system.

I first worked in this city when Dwight Eisenhower was president. I was a young lawyer then, and there are some who say I have recovered from both conditions. I was invited by Ray Jenkins to be an unpaid staff person for the Army McCarthy Hearings, and that was my real exposure to Washington. Although my father served in the House of Representatives for a long time, that was my first total immersion into the hearing process and to the U.S. Senate.

But in any event, I came here when Dwight Eisenhower was president, I was elected to the Senate when Lyndon Johnson was president, and I was privileged to be the Majority Leader of the Senate when Ronald Reagan was president. With this background, it was nothing less than extraordinary to see a president feel obliged to plead his relevance to the government of which he is chief executive. And yet I can understand what impels him to protest his relevance.

An electorate insistent on change elects him in 1992, then repudiates him in 1994, and effectively ignores him in 1995 as it gets better acquainted with the new political system, with the Senate and especially with the House that Newt built.

I feel a certain sense of déjà vu because the same sort of thing was happening thirty years ago when I was first elected to the Senate from Tennessee. Lyndon Johnson had been elected president two years earlier, in 1964, and he bestrode this city as no one had done since Franklin Roosevelt. Yet only two years later the president and his party suffered a striking defeat at the polls, with Republicans gaining 47 seats in the House and sending an attractive class of young Senators to Washington with names like Hatfield, Percy, Griffin, Hansen, and Brooke.

We of the Class of 1966 had not committed ourselves to any common agenda. There was nothing like the Contract with America then, but what we did have in common was a belief that the policies of the Johnson Administration were beginning to injure the economy and inflame the passions of the people of this country in a dangerous and destructive way.

We came to Washington at a time when American cities, including this one, were erupting in violence with alarming frequency. We came here when political assassinations were becoming almost commonplace, with President Kennedy, Malcolm X, Martin Luther King, and Robert Kennedy all murdered within the space of five years.

It was no sentimental thing for us to embrace the politics of civility, anchored in a belief that whatever our political differences in this country, we should be able to lower our voices, to control our passions and try to find a political consensus to deal with the problems that so vexed our society. This devotion to civility, which was a measure of strength then, is sometimes disdained as a weakness now. Politicians who try to work across party lines are dismissed as accommodationists and trimmers. Motives as well as methods are subject to vigorous challenge. Republicans—so long in the wilderness, so ill treated in their exile—are hard pressed to find a generous word to say about their Democratic colleagues, and the ill favor is returned in kind.

It is easy enough and it may even be right to say that in times like this, when we are debating such fundamental questions as the proper role and size of the federal government, it is more important to be clear than to be kind, better to draw distinctions than to compose differences.

But I think we endanger something even more fundamental—the underlying goodwill of a free society—when we refuse to acknowledge that our political opponents have any redeeming value at all. That attitude takes politics too far and makes the difficult job of governing very nearly impossible.

I admire Lloyd Cutler because he understands this requirement for fundamental civility in the conflict of ideas and the contest for the support of the people of this country. Lloyd and I have been undoubted activists on behalf of our parties and on behalf of our ideas. And we have often clashed, sometimes in very visible ways. But I find it difficult to conceive of a situation where we would be personally disagreeable on those issues, recognizing that there is merit in the other's point of view. I admire people like him on both sides of the aisle who understand the essence of the art of governance.

The political heirs of Ronald Reagan who now control the Congress would do well to remember that President Reagan, who loved a good political fight as much as anybody, loved people more. As an example he counted Tip O'Neill, with whom he had vociferous disagreements, as a personal friend.

The successors to John F. Kennedy and Lyndon Johnson who now inhabit the White House would do well to recall that those men knew the value of bipartisanship and understood that a Douglas Dillon in their cabinet or an Everett Dirksen on their side in a legislative cause was a sign of strength and not a sign of weakness.

I fear there is too much institutional animus between the presidency and Congress in these days, no matter who occupies the seats of power. From budget policy to war powers, everything has become a test of institutional prerogatives as well as political will. There is little wonder then that this churlish display of political animus turns off Americans by the millions. It is not the sole reason that Americans do not vote in massive numbers, as our friends in Europe and Asia do, but it is part of the reason.

We are almost certainly in the midst of an historic adjustment of the roles of the executive and the legislative branches of our federal government. Such adjustments seem to come every few decades in our history, often in response to external events, but also in the gathering up of the collective demand by the people of this country that we do things differently.

The end of the cold war is certainly one of the defining events that drives our citizenry to demand something different. The primacy of the presidency in an era of apocalyptic danger may be giving way to the ascendancy of Congress in an age when we are safe enough to turn our attention to issues of federalism, function, and finance.

But as the tragedy of Oklahoma City has shown us anew, there are strains of extremism and violence in this country that we must take care not to nourish.

I do not think anything good came out of Oklahoma City. I think it was an unmitigated disaster. It is unimaginable that the mind of man can conceive of such an event and carry it out.

And whether it was an offshoot of an underground militia or not does not matter. I do not think conservative, or liberal, or moderate matters. I think that it points up one fact: you must have social structures that can accommodate the challenge of crazy people who will do outrageous things.

I think the country is going to demand some level of moderation in our public discourse—some attenuation of its grosser aspects—and on both sides. Oklahoma City may contribute to that. One reason for government, an effective government, is that there are people like that, and they have to be dealt with.

A Congress that finds nothing good to say about government, or an administration that cynically links extremism with conservatism, is playing with fire in this age of anger and alienation. And having seen these forces loosed on this country before, and having seen, then and now, the terrible price we pay for it, I hope we can tone down the rhetoric, lower our voices, and remember—as Lincoln taught us, and as the good people of Oklahoma City remind us—that we are not enemies, but friends. We must not be our own enemies.

There are many things wrong with our government, but there are many more that are right. It is our job in life, as citizens, to build on the good—to improve it and to go forward so that our country's greatest days lie always ahead of us rather than behind us.

... Of the People toward Their Government

Lloyd N. Cutler

One of Howard Baker's finest acts, I think, was when he helped President Carter to obtain the approval of the Panama Canal Treaty by one vote. It was the kind of controversial issue on which his position could well have made a difference in his quest for the presidential nomination a few years later. But Howard Baker thought it was the right thing to do and he stood by. It was the kind of issue that Clark Clifford described as one you should wait to bring up until the third year of your second term. But President Carter, being a man of principle also, did it in his first and only term, and Howard stood right with him and helped him get it done.

I have been working on these issues of reforming government to lessen deadlock. I recently watched Judge Bill Schwartzer receive an award for being chairman of the Federal Judicial Council, and he was being praised for all the reforms he had accomplished in the judicial system. He referred first to the British Parliamentary leader at the time of the Reform Act who said, "Reform? Why do we want reform? Things are bad enough as they are."

We are older and wiser after thirteen years of talking about the constitutional system. But I would rather discuss here the question that such a large percentage of our voters mistrust and distrust public officials and institutions regardless of which party and which individuals are in power.

Poll after poll shows widespread distrust of government, at least at the national level. Public service was once supposed to be a noble calling, but many today think that anyone who is willing to run for federal office or accept a federal appointment is either a knave or a fool, and perhaps both. And I referring to a distrust and disdain that goes beyond mere disappointment with the decisions and the nondecisions and deadlocks of government.

All of us are concerned about the frustrations and the hazards of our lives, and we have an understandable tendency to blame the government, or consequences of technological developments, or social changes concerning which the government may promise much but can really do very little about.

We distrust government much more than our neighbors, the Canadians, who share our social and economic background, and even our television, but who continue to believe as we once did that government is part of the solution, not part of the problem.

What is truly different today is the degree to which we now blame government and government officials for our continuing discontent. You all know about the polls. A *Los Angeles Times* Center survey of voter attitudes found that the percentage dissatisfied with the way things are going in the country rose steadily from 40 percent in October 1988 to 68 percent in January 1992. That was still during the Bush administration. There was a little rise in confidence when President Clinton was elected, but followed by a rise in the dissatisfaction to more than 70 percent in 1993 and 1994. Over 70 percent believe that elected officials in Washington lose touch with the people pretty quickly. Only 25 percent feel that those we send to Washington try hard to stay in touch with people back home, and 65 percent feel that most elected officials do not care what people like us think. Obviously this goes far beyond the militias that we are concerned about today. And an exit poll conducted for the *New York Times* on Election Day 1994 confirmed those same results. That explains the manifestation of 1992, when 19 percent of the people voted for a nonparty candidate, Ross Perot.

Jefferson's maxim that government is best when it governs least is becoming more popular every day, even among the young who depend on government loans for their higher education, and the old who depend on government social security and medicare payments at levels far beyond the amounts that they personally have contributed to the system.

Now there is, of course, much to be admired in the qualities of self-reliance and skepticism about "Big Brother" that account for this growing disdain for public institutions. But there is much less to admire in the growing public disdain for the persons who serve us as elected or appointed public officials, and there is no sign at all that I can see, that a healthier balance will soon be reached.

There is an ironic fallacy to all of this. In my experience—and I have been around quite a while—the public officials of today, elected and appointed, are unquestionably better educated, more highly principled, more thoroughly vetted, more decent and competent than their predecessors of thirty, forty, and fifty years ago, when public respect for public officials was considerably higher than it is today. I can remember days of plain white envelopes full of cash being passed in House and Senate offices and in the White House itself, with no paper trail of who gave the money or what the quid pro quo was. There were no laws governing campaign financing or the acceptance of political gifts, or conflicts of interest on either side of the revolving door. And yet, as the quality and the behavior of public officials has been steadily improving, the public's general respect for its public servants has turned into general disdain.

We have moved from distrust of the bureaucracy—best expressed in the aphorism of the day that "we're the government and we're here to help you"—to distrust of Congress, culminating in the current term limits extravaganza and the popular notion that time in Congress is more or less equivalent to serving time in jail, and that with three strikes, as in the case of a criminal, you're out. Now we have turned on the White House and whoever happens to be its incumbent. And while we focus today on President Clinton, it is well to remember that President Bush, after achieving a 90 percent approval rating immediately after the Persian Gulf War, never rose above 38 percent in the crucial 1992 campaign, even during the couple of months when Ross Perot had taken himself out of the race.

And think of what we now do to people who run for president or serve on the president's staff. Before election or appointment, we subject them to the most minute examination of their entire personal lives, including their financial status and transactions, the reports of their neighbors anywhere they ever lived, their personal habits, their medical histories (including whether they ever consulted a psychiatrist), and their tax status (including withholding taxes for their household help). And the final vetting question asks whether there is literally anything that might prove embarrassing to a potential appointee or to the president if generally known.

Vetting was part of my responsibility as President Clinton's counsel.

Although we made a lot of reforms, the process is so overlayered and so detailed that I made a calculation that the president could not possibly finish filling all the vacancies he had to fill before the end of his term. And then, when our officials finally are elected or appointed, they run a very high risk (getting higher every day) of having to undergo one or more independent counsel or congressional investigations for which they will need to retain a private lawyer. They have to retain a lawyer because under our laws any government lawyer cannot maintain the attorney-client privilege if he or she represents another government official. If the lawyer hears anything that indicates evidence of a violation of the law, it must be reported to the Department of Justice.

This need to hire a lawyer arises not only for the target of an investigation (let's say a Mike Espy) but also for people who are simply wanted as witnesses. Any lawyer, or anyone who has served in the government, know that the biggest no-no of all is to think you can handle it yourself and go before a grand jury or a congressional investigation inquiring into your own personal conduct, or what you overheard in a meeting, without being prepared by your own lawyer.

This is what happened to President Reagan and to Vice President Bush in the Iran-Contra investigation, in which both had to disclose their personal diaries to the independent counsel. It happened again to President Bush in the Clinton passport investigation, where again his diaries had to be made available to the independent counsel. And it happened to President Clinton in the Whitewater case, where he voluntarily agreed to the request for depositions before the independent counsel. Fortunately, he never kept a diary.

None of the three was ever a subject or target of these investigations. They were merely witnesses. And in the Whitewater investigations, some fifteen or twenty White House and Treasury officials were called to testify three to five times each by the independent counsel or a congressional committee relating to contacts about the RTC referral of the Madison Guaranty matter. Most of them were mere witnesses, yet all had to retain private counsel and pay legal fees, in some cases amounting to half or more of their meager government salaries.

This same need to hire a private lawyer at great expense has been imposed on two cabinet secretaries in this administration and members of their staff. This is not just a Clinton administration phenomenon; it happened to at least six Reagan and Bush Cabinet secretaries—to

Attorney General Meese three times, to Secretary Donovan, Secretary Shultz, Secretary Weinberger, Secretary Pierce, and Secretary Baker. I happened to represent both Secretary Shultz and Secretary Baker, so I know how much this cost. It also happened to CIA Director Casey and White House aides Donald Regan, Michael Deaver, and Lyn Nofziger, during the Reagan and Bush administrations.

With these high personal and financial costs of public service, how many parents are left in the country who want their sons or daughters to grow up to be president, a member of Congress, or a high-level government official?

When the Philadelphia Constitutional Convention ended, a journalist came up to Benjamin Franklin, who was the leading highly placed anonymous source on what went on inside the convention's closed doors. The journalist asked, "Mr. Franklin, what have we got?" And Franklin was said to have answered, "A republic, if you can keep it." My question to you today is whether we are in danger of losing our capacity to keep it. Can we still govern this complex, rapidly changing nation and lead the rest of the world toward peace, democracy, and economic growth, if our growing disdain and vilification of public officials make us unable to attract the very best among us—the Howard Bakers among us—to devote at least a part of their careers to public service? As much as I have been interested in political structure and political strategy, I now think this is the greatest question that faces us today.

Does the System
Need Fixing?

"It Ain't Broke . . ."

Charles O. Jones

The source of my title, is, of course, the pithy aphorism: "If it ain't broke, don't fix it." I would add this advisory: "If it is broke, choose your fixer carefully—and always get a second opinion." It is a quality of a separated powers system like ours that it always appears broken, thus encouraging professional fixers to ply their trade. Some political systems work with "clean" theories—the most pristine of which have proven to be very wrong. We dirty things up a bit by promoting access, propagating legitimate participation, and dispersing accountability, yet compelling agreement. None of it works very well, as Barber Conable has observed, "just as the founding fathers intended." The separated system doesn't show well along the way.

The stimulus to make changes in our political system often derives from a desire to have presidential government and strong political parties in the parliamentary mode. Congress gets in the way of achieving this end and is therefore the subject of much criticism and many reform proposals. The president should be strong, policy ambitious, and responsible so that he can form a government—well, at least those we agree with should be so endowed. The system at present is viewed as producing gridlock, a term applied when either the president or the House or the Senate exercises their constitutional prerogatives to check the other branch.

It is surely true that serious participation in a separated system is big-time politics. Not everyone is good at it—some, in fact, should seek other employment. Surely we know by now that partisanship is not sufficient. Consider how Madison and the lads disconnected the elections

71

and varied the term lengths. House members who came in with the president are on their own in two years time. The one-third of the Senate elected with the president will never again see him on the ballot.

Therefore, most of the time presidents have to work hard to form cross-party coalitions, to convince members of Congress that what they want is good for them and their constituents. Ours is not a partisan, party-based system. Those who try to manage on a partisan basis typically fail. Nor do party members fall neatly into policy slots. And so cross-party coalitions on one issue may look very different from those on other issues. Building support is continuous. It requires that legitimate interests be heard and that deals then be made.

Otto von Bismarck is believed to have said: "If you like laws and sausages, you should never watch either one being made." That is fine for sausage, and probably for laws the way Bismarck made them. But that is nonsense for us. Take a look—a good look. Others do. Ours is the most watched system in the world, and should be. What you don't like can be changed only with your attention and participation—not with turning away. And instituting a system based on "clean" theory would do more harm than help.

One feature of a separated system that troubles critics is the potential for divided government or, as I prefer to label it, split-party government. If it is difficult to form a government in the parliamentary sense when one party has won the White House, the House of Representatives, and the Senate, then imagine the problems when each party wins a branch of government. First it is worth observing that such an outcome is a perfectly constitutional result, not a perversion. Then it is notable that voters have, in this age of modern, electronic communication, returned split-party government a majority of the time. When asked, they even profess a preference for that outcome.

Has split-party government resulted in gridlock? Not if measured by the production of major legislation, according to David R. Mayhew in his book *Divided We Govern*. There is no difference between single- and split-party government by his count. In fact, one of the most productive periods was 1973–74, when we believed at the time that government had virtually ceased to work because of Watergate.

My own detailed study of major legislation during the post–World War II period shows a rich variety of presidential-congressional interaction at all stages of lawmaking, with initiative coming from both parties and from all three elected institutions. Why should we not expect that variation in a scheme that propagates legitimate involvement by duly and independently elected representatives?

What about the system in the next century? I believe it will be more like it is and has been than what many want it to be. Reforms will be put in place, to be sure—many were in this Congress. But present students of American politics will have no trouble recognizing their government twenty years from now. It will continue to be a separated system of diffused responsibility, broad access, institutional and federal-state competition, and cross-party alliances on issues. The strong party, presidency-centered advocates will be just as frustrated then as they are now, perhaps more so.

None of that is to say that the partisan balances will be the same. The 1994 elections resulted in a stunning reshuffling of power; displaying another variation is separated system politics. I will say something about those results since it is my belief that much is to be learned about the future from what is happening in the present.

One can sympathize with the President Clinton as he struggles to find his place in the revised politics of the day. The president lost an election without being on the ballot—the only first-term elected Democrat in this century to lose both houses of Congress (Truman was not an elected president in 1946). He is experiencing what no Republican president could arrange over the past forty years—a Republican majority in the House. His present status and strategic options are defined by the congressional Republicans—not an enviable position. And so President Clinton has had to reshape a presidency that was not that well formed from the start, a challenge to cope with a rare form of split-party government.

But there is more that is historic. American political parties are criticized in presidential elections for offering, then ignoring, relatively flaccid party platforms. We surely don't expect to have explicit contracts with the voters during the state and local contests that make up a congressional midterm election.

In fact, despite the preference among many analysts for the strong party model of government, many were puzzled by Newt Gingrich's media extravaganza on September 27 when he brought House Republican candidates to Capitol Hill to. sign the Contract with America. David Broder was one of the few commentators to recognize the effort as suited to party government: "Newt Gingrich . . . said at a press briefing, 'Our government operates on the party system. We are

a team. And we're offering you a contract on what our team will do.'
. . . That is a sound proposition. People need to be reminded that
Congress writes the laws in a partisan setting . . . in which the
opposing parties divide, not just for spite, but on philosophy, program
and principle" (*Washington Post*, September 28, 1994, p. A23).

Most analysts were skeptical, if not mocking, of the exercise. E. J.
Dionne reported: "Many Democratic strategists are gleeful because
this document ties 'outsider' Republican candidates back into their
congressional leadership and defines the Republicans as advocates of
tattered Reagan-style tax cuts." Stanley Greenberg, Clinton's pollster,
was quoted by Dionne as stating that the Republicans had made a mistake with the Contract in offering policy substance that was not popular (*Washington Post,* October 4, 1994, p. A17).

Paul Begala was quoted in the *New York Times* as very pleased with
the Contract: "There is not a night I don't thank God for the contract"
(October 9, 1994, p. A26). Editorial comment was scathing: "Reaganism
in a rear-view mirror," "reckless," "deceptive," "duplicitous propa-
ganda," "a gimmick." (*New York Times*, September 28, 1994, p. A20;
Washington Post, September 28, 1994, p. A22).

Studies by my colleagues in political science will no doubt show
that the Contract played a minor role with voters in the 1994 elections.
In other respects, however, it was an historic development. A huge
majority of Republican candidates signed the document and took it
seriously. And tying "outsider" candidates into their congressional
leadership is exactly what Gingrich and Co. had in mind as support for
their consolidation of power in potential competition with new committee chairs.

Because much of reality is perceptual, the fact that House
Republicans did much better than expected was bound to encourage
talk of a mandate, that goofy concept for a separated system that is
used in postelection analysis to make sense of what typically is not
there. In this case the mandate was awarded to a leader who was very
anxious to act.

The third historic aspect of the 104th Congress is in what was
accomplished early. The House Republicans accomplished all of what
they promised in the Contract—that is, to bring to a vote all of the legislative actions listed therein. More than that, they passed the overwhelming majority of the proposals brought to the floor within the
time limit they set and with extraordinary party unity. Still more, they

created an energy and momentum that is unprecedented for so early in a session. A president accomplishing this much in the first three months would have been labeled a political genius.

Is this a case of the effective working of the separated system? It is not. One-hundred-day deadlines are not well suited to our policy politics. Scorekeeping becomes an end in itself. There is a probable inverse relationship between a high score and good legislation. To say that the House Republicans achieved, even exceeded, the goals set in the Contract is not necessarily to point with pride to the results. Legislation by exhaustion is not recommended, nor is urgent large-scale testing of grand behavioral and structural theories of governing.

The House Republicans set an impressive agenda in this first one hundred days—one directed to basic questions about what government can do, which government ought to do it, as well as the capacity of the private sphere to solve public problems. It is surely the envy of any policy-ambitious president. But speculation abounds as to whether these will be the effects of political reform and policy change:

—Term limits will improve lawmaking.

—Denial of cash benefits will reduce teenage pregnancies.

—Block grants to the states will reduce bureaucracy.

—States are better at governing than is the nation.

—The item veto will reduce unnecessary expenditures.

—Cost-benefit analysis of regulations will limit government control.

—Capping punitive damages lowers medical care costs.

—"Loser pays" will reduce the number of frivolous lawsuits.

—Tax cuts are consistent with balancing the budget.

—A constitutional amendment will produce a balanced budget.

The quantity and complexity of legislation passed by the House and sent to the Senate in the first three months were awesome. The legislative pipeline was full even before the budget debates began. The House voted on final passage on twenty-six pieces of legislation—twenty-five wins and one loss.

Of these twenty votes on final passage, Republicans lost an average of 6 votes per bill (a range of 0 to 40, on term limits). They picked up an average of 83 Democratic votes (a range of 6 to 201). Party unity for House Republicans averaged 97 percent for the 26 votes (with a range of from 83 to 100 percent). Just one vote—term limits—fell below 90 percent unity. Republicans had 99 to 100 percent unity on 12 of the votes.

What is frightening about this record? Should we not be overjoyed that party government is here at last? It was precisely this type of law-making that concerned the Founders. Big questions have been answered by untested theories and with little time devoted to considering the consequences.

It is, indeed, a time for considering major shifts to achieve effectiveness of government at all levels. But in our system, devolution is to be achieved by evolution, not revolution.

That brings me to the reassurance offered by a separated system. Speaker Gingrich likes to compare this period with that in 1933. Indeed, the lamentable one-hundred-day timetable emanates from that time. Democratic presidents are fond of invoking the one-hundred-day promise; President Clinton being the most recent example with his economic and health care proposals. So far as I am aware, this is the first time a congressional leader has proposed such an ambitious program on this schedule. And he did it.

The argument for acting quickly is familiar. President Johnson summarized it well in his memoirs: "A president must always reckon that his mandate will prove short-lived." He might have added, "because it wasn't real anyway."

The separated system was sure to kick in. The House Republicans seized the initiative in setting the agenda and in formulating proposals that were fed to the other elected institutions. This is no small achievement—it is historic, as I have already pointed out.

Whereas the Senate will abide by this agenda for the most part, it will function precisely as designed. Counterproposals will be developed, action will be more deliberate, the minority party will be substantially more influential in forcing compromises, alternative theories will be propounded to those used as a basis for bills in the House, senators will take time to display their plumage.

And representatives of the two chambers will then meet in conference when passions have cooled.

I stress again the importance of the role played by Speaker Gingrich and the House Republicans. But a mandate for one of the three elected institutions is very different from one assigned to all three as led by the president (for example, 1932, 1964, and 1980). Just as the president is not the presidency and the presidency is not the government, just so the Speaker is not the House and the House is not the government (or even Congress).

What of the president's role in this version of the separated system? Of course, it depends on the person serving in the Oval Office. A president with limited domestic policy goals or one whose goals have been achieved (such as Eisenhower or Reagan in their final two years or Bush virtually from the start) can accommodate rather well to these political circumstances. They can concentrate on foreign and national security matters, employ the veto to curb congressional excesses, and participate in domestic initiatives where political gain might be realized.

For a policy-ambitious president like Bill Clinton, however, there can be no greater predicament than to have lost control of the agenda. After all, reactive presidents are not listed among the great leaders. And, seemingly, his political operatives were not prepared for a worst-case scenario. A garrulous president was made nearly speechless.

Since election day, however, a White House strategy has emerged that accommodates the new politics. As revealed in his December 15 speech on taxes, the State of the Union Message, and the subsequent speech in Dallas, the principal tenets appear to be these:

—Associate the president with the change seemingly demanded by the voters. Argue that the 1994 results represent a continuation of the mandate for change designated as a consequence of the 1992 election.

—Remind the public that the president was there first with many of the issues of the Contract with America—tax cuts, welfare reform, relief for the states, reducing the deficit—and he will thus be cooperative where possible.

—Reveal that the president's proposals are more humane—they represent improving government, not destroying it. Thus he will identify the limits of devolution to the states, measuring proposals by their adverse effects on various clienteles.

—Threaten the veto primarily as a means for identifying the president's position. Avoid being too specific before more explicit Senate action for strategic reasons.

—State a "no politics-as-usual" position—getting it right is more important than being reelected.

—Take full advantage of the uniquely presidential status in foreign and national security issues, as well as national disasters or crises.

Taken overall, this constitutes a defensible strategy for a weakened presidency. It represents an effort to reestablish a basis for participating, perhaps for regaining an initiative in policymaking. The preparations have been made, carefully and strategically. Much now depends on whether Republicans can maintain the unity displayed in the first one hundred days and attract sufficient Democratic support to remain in control of the lawmaking process. Either way, what we are observing is less an aberration than a mutation in the pliant separated system.

I close with these thoughts from a great and honored public servant:

> Perhaps the dominant feeling about government today is distrust. The tone of most comment, whether casual or deliberate, implies that ineptitude and inadequacy are the chief characteristics of government. I do not refer merely to the current skepticism about democracy, but to the widely entertained feeling of the incapacity of government, generally, to satisfy the needs of modern society. But . . . we ask more from government than any society has ever asked. At one and the same time, we expect little from government and progressively rely on it more. We feel that the essential forces of life are no longer in the channels of politics, and yet we constantly turn to those channels for the direction of forces outside them. Generalizations like these elude proof because they are usually based on very subtle factors. But the large abstention from voting in our elections must certainly bespeak an indifference not without meaning. . . . We have not adjusted our thinking about government to the overwhelming facts of modern life, and so carry over old mental habits, traditional schoolbook platitudes and campaign slogans as to the role, the purposes, and the methods of government.

These words are a part of my reassurance. As contemporary as they sound, they were in fact delivered by Felix Frankfurter in a lecture sixty-five years ago this month. We ain't fixed yet, Mr. Justice, and probably never will be. But we ain't hopelessly broke either; and whatever we do by way of repairs, we need to be careful not to interfere too much with the current national conversation about government and its role in our lives. With regard to the structure of the separated system, be assured that the Founders built in sufficient protections to preserve even its most maddening features.

The 1990s'
Political Upheaval
and the
Pressures for Reform

Kevin P. Phillips

To borrow a social analogy, I think I am the skunk at the garden party. There has been a lot of reaffirmation—a lot of angst-free assurances that the system that has got militias organizing in twenty states is in fact doing very well. I will suggest that it is not. The evidence of the malfunction and the disillusionment of the public, and the extent to which a lot of these trends are paralleled elsewhere among the G-7 nations, is really of quite considerable significance.

Washington is malfunctioning in three particular dimensions: the difficult relationship of overly separated powers; the enormous buildup and entrenchment of the largest interest group concentration the world has ever seen; and a Republican and Democratic two-party system that no longer adequately appeals to the electorate.

Over the next fifteen years or so the remedies (or I suppose more often the *attempts*) to change are likely to include more independent and third-party national campaigns, more direct or participatory democracy, and some new twenty-first century variety of national identification and voter qualification system. I am not sure what it will be. But it will be linked to the problems of coping with immigration and with the soaring cost of entitlements, and the need to get all of these things under control in ways that technology does now begin to make possible, as well as the likelihood that something in this vein can also become a national registry that could considerably enlarge the electorate.

I think that we are going to have a number of reforms develop around these various contexts. Now obviously there is a lot of room to move off in different ways, but basically I think a lot of this is in the cards.

But first let me turn to some essential circumstances. The details of some of this have been spelled out in a book I published in the fall of 1994, *Arrogant Capital*, the title referring both to Washington and Wall Street, the derivatives and the derivators. I will give a quick sketch of the factors that I think are either linked to the malfunctioning in Washington or that reflect the public's deep-seated and continuing alienation.

First, there is the extraordinary buildup in interest groups. I don't agree with the people who emphasize payrolls in the government and the change over the last half-century. To be sure, there is a problem with congressional staff going from 3,000 in 1945 to about 20,000 now. But much more important changes, the critical explosion, has come in the private and nonprofit sectors, where there has been an enormous burgeoning. In 1945 this city had perhaps a couple of thousand lobbyists and other persons involved in supporting lobbying activities; according to James Thurber at American University, there are now 91,000 people who are lobbyists or engaged in supporting lobbying activity. This presumably includes the librarian at the National Association of Snowmobile Dealers. But in terms of the basic thrust of what's happened in this city, I think this number is absolutely right.

The number of people admitted to the bar, or the federal court of the District of Columbia, has gone from about 1,000 in 1950 to about 61,000 today. And of course, we have an enormous percentage of the international bar, the tax bar, the patent and copyright bar, and others here in Washington.

Partly as a result of this incredible expansion, metropolitan Washington now has seven of the top twenty U.S. counties in terms of per capita income. That's a fascinating statistic in itself, because here is the city that was famous back in the 1930s for mixing Northern charm and Southern efficiency, and in came a huge crop of professionals that made this is the most affluent concentration of professional workers in the country. At a time when many Americans don't feel that they are sharing in national affluence, they know Washington is.

The second point is that this interest group structure is tightly interlocked with the two-party system. I think any examination of the party system has to look at the extent to which interest groups have grown up and interlocked with it, which creates a kind of double-edged problem, the one reinforcing the other. Service in the two-party system is what punches professional tickets in Washington. Whether it be from party committees, or the U.S. Trade Representatives office, or any other positions of substance, essentially public office has become a training ground for private profit in all too many cases.

The influence of this interlock has been so strong recently that in the last Congress, for the first time I can remember, two senior members of the House resigned when major lobbying jobs became available. They didn't just wait to retire—they switched positions. We used to talk about lobbyists as the fourth branch of government, but clearly in the last couple of decades they have gone up a notch or two. The result is that when a new president or a new Congress comes to town—Democrat or Republican, 1992 or 1994—the shriveling of anti-Washington campaign rhetoric begins, and they are soon cutting deals with the people they attacked and often asking for checks in return.

What has happened here is that such an extraordinary interest group concentration has built up in this city that when a new administration or a new Congress of either party comes to town, it is like iron filings dropping into the field of an electromagnet. Whatever they promised in Paducah, when they get here they know who writes the checks and who has the offices on K Street and who represents the people who count. True, there's a lot of interest in what people think back in Paducah; but unfortunately all too often that isn't what drives legislators in the crunch.

As far as the third point to underscore, the growth of this system has been most striking over the last thirty years—not the growth in the number of federal employees, because that came earlier, but the growth in the private and nonprofit sector, where the real salaries are paid and the real money is made, and the real incomes are earned that put seven out of the top twenty U.S. counties in metropolitan Washington. When Tiffany's took their first branch out of Manhattan, they put it in Fairfax County. They didn't go to King of Prussia, Pennsylvania, and they didn't go to Brookline, Massachusetts—they came down here to Government and Interest Group Central.

If we go back and look at the last thirty years and the statistics of what the public thinks of Washington, you can see that the peak came more or less in the early 1960s. Then, 75 or 76 percent of Americans said you could always or usually trust Washington. That's not the case anymore. I'll come back to some other numbers, but that statistic is down to 19 or 20 percent, and incidentally it hasn't changed from last year to this.

When *Time* magazine excerpted my book *Arrogant Capital* last September, they ran two dozen national poll questions to test what people thought about all these relationships. And, of course, people think that Washington is run by the special interests—no big surprise there. Sixty-one percent said it wasn't enough to change the faces; you had to change the system. When respondents were asked if George Washington would be proud of Washington, D.C., or disappointed, just 7 percent said he would be proud, while 86 percent say he would have been disappointed.

This anger was part of what helped the Republicans take over Congress in the last election. But the new Republican Congress has perceived a different and in some ways I think parochial mandate for conservative ideology and economics, and in the case of the House of Representatives, for an unprecedented collaboration and closeness with the special interest lobbies. It's almost as if they are being delegated aspects of the legislative function in the House.

As for the one thing that was the highest priority of the public (and especially Republican independent voters in the polls)—term limits—that's the one, of course, that fell through the cracks.

And so, according to the spring poll, 60 to 65 percent of the American people still see politics as usual. Lack of trust of Washington is still at those 1994 levels—just 20 percent, according to a recent *ABC News–Washington Post* poll believe they can trust government most or all of the time. The new Speaker of the House has personal credibility ratings below those of the also-unpopular President. April's *Times-Mirror Poll* found, in a record for that particular poll, that 57 percent of Americans now want a third party. That includes half the Republicans—hardly a trumpet salute to the first one hundred days. It is time that the political and opinion-molding classes in this country face up to these malfunctions in the public distrust that they have bred.

Before I discuss some of the possible reforms, it is also appropriate to note a second set of circumstances—in this case, some related patterns and remedies in the other G-7 nations, and the lessons that we might take from them.

To begin with, the weaknesses being shown by the existing party system in the United States have a lot of parallels elsewhere. The unraveling of the last three or four years has been striking. In Italy and Japan the old systems have virtually come unglued. It was evident in the distress of all the parties in Japan at the recent mayoralty elections in Osaka and Tokyo, where they elected TV personalities who had been clowns on television. (I guess they decided to go straight to what they think politics represents.) Needless to say, this has made a considerable number of Japanese politicians quite unhappy.

In Germany, contempt for the political system has produced a new word to describe it: *Politikverdrossenheit.*

In Canada the Progressive Conservatives, who were the government in the 1993 election, declined from 155 members of Parliament to two. They now no longer have official status. They were passed by the Quebec separatists and the Reform Party in Alberta, which is the across-the-border Perotistas.

In France, if we examine the election results we saw recently, they obviously reflect the balkanization taking place there.

In Britain, the state of the Conservative Party is so bad that they control the local council in only one shire, Buckinghamshire, and they're in big trouble even there. Pundits are writing in the *Financial Times* and the London Sunday papers that the Tories may have to watch out for a Canadian-type result.

It is hardly surprising in light of all this that Americans find their two-party system isn't worth much and that 57 percent told the *Times-Mirror* poll a couple of weeks ago that they wanted a new party. People don't agree on which party. But that has to be a central part of the discussion of where the U.S. party system is about to go. We not only have these indications and discontents, but they are also reflected in the way in which the other countries in the post–cold war period have basically given a thumbs-down on the old parties they tolerated or voted for so long before all that readjustment.

Propping up the Republicans and Democrats in this country should be a debate. It should not be an assumption—not anymore.

A second international parallel involves the American electorate's overwhelming demand for the establishment of a national referendum mechanism. When *Time* ran its special poll on the ideas in *Arrogant Capital,* they found such a mechanism was supported 76 percent to 19 percent—a margin of four to one, a record, and the highest number that question has gotten. It used to be only 50 to 60 percent of voters favored the idea of voting on key national issues. This demand is not only obvious here, but there is also a trend in the other English-speaking countries.

In Britain just a couple of years ago, Margaret Thatcher wanted a nationwide vote on European monetary unification. John Major has made similar hints. The Labour Party talks about having a nationwide referendum on electoral reforms. If they decide to dump the House of Lords in favor of establishing a Senate, they would probably put in some form of proportional representation. It is still a big question whether the political elite would ever take that direction in the House of Commons, because of the way it would have of building up the Liberal Democrats. But if Labour needs the Liberal Democrats after the next election, there could be proportional representation there. In any event, whatever electoral reform they do will probably be done by a referendum.

In Canada they had a referendum on the status of Quebec a couple of years ago. In Australia they have referenda all the time. In a referendum about a year ago, New Zealand voted to change from its first-past-the-post, winner-take-all system in legislative districts to proportional representation. The rest of the English-speaking world has already moved much more than we have on this referendum aspect nationally.

In terms of what all this is likely to add up to, I think what it reflects is stress on the old English-speaking system that involved, in our case alone, single separation of powers, but in *every* case, first-past-the-post systems, and in earlier years and eras two-party systems. It is really beginning to splinter. The likelihood is that it will move more in the directions of other countries. I could add South Africa to that list, although it is probably not illustrative; but there again, we see referenda, switching to proportional representation.

With technology facilitating all of this, I think it's inevitable that we have certain degrees of national citizen voting on key issues. The question is, what? Let me turn to some individual proposals here, some relatively specific and some quite vague.

First, to deal with the problem of concentrated power in Washington, there is something to be said for the Howard Baker–Lamar Alexander proposal for a citizen legislature that spends only six months a year in Washington and then goes home. Technology clearly makes it possible to have more and more politicking and even congressional activity done in a "Virtual Washington" situation that could take place in districts. There have been proposals to let people vote in their home districts in case of emergency or illness in the family or whatever, and the leadership killed it several years ago. But again, that proposal is something that will likely recur. As people want influences brought to bear on the politicians to come back to the grassroots, one thing to do is get the politicians to spend more time in Wawatosa and less time on Wall Street or K Street, and I think people will push that.

The question of term limits has been belabored enough. I do not really believe it will pass in Washington. But it would be interesting to take note of one of the arguments against term limits—namely, that applying them to the politicians will be giving power to the staff and to the lobbyists. Any term limitation on the politicians should be accompanied by a 30, 40, 50, or 60 percent cutback in the personal and committee staffs. The new GOP leadership did not touch the personal staffs in any meaningful way. I have my own little hobby horse here—how about term limits for lobbyists? Suppose they had to be issued tickets, so to speak, and no one could have a ticket for more than eight years. But this would probably not be constitutional, alas.

In terms of sheer delight, imagine that just when somebody has worked up to be a real hired gun—able to slip all kinds of garbage into the tax code, to set a waiver on this and an exception for that—the law sends that individual back to Sheboygan. Don't just send the officeholders back, send the other influence-mongers back too. I think a case can even be made for term limits on journalists. A lot of politicians and a lot of voters would support that one.

To be more specific on direct democracy, what we have to think about is some kind of national referendum mechanism. Why is it that of all the English-speaking countries, we alone don't have any kind of national referendum? Now the answer some give—that maybe our electorate is the least trustworthy—isn't something that anyone would want to voice as a reason. However, if this were to be set up, it would have to be established with the same kind of limited jurisdiction that might exist in Canada or in Britain, where they vote on something like Maastricht or Quebec, or in New Zealand, where they vote on major electoral reforms. We shouldn't open, for example, with referenda on tax changes. Switzerland does that very well, but it's unrealistic to assume that we could start out with something like that and not court disaster.

However, with a very limited jurisdiction, the sort of things that the British and Canadians put up for national referenda, Americans would have a chance to start getting involved, and I think that would probably sit very well with the public. Polls in the last few weeks have showed that voters in huge numbers would like the country to be able to vote on the items in the Contract with America. Even if they don't like it, they'd like to be able to vote on it. That's so much of a disassociation from interest group—run Washington that the public will take back anything they can get.

The two-party system as it presently exists is not going to last. Part of that is because we are not going to need parties much in the twenty-first century. We will need groupings, but these will probably call for substantially different mechanisms. I agree this will come more slowly than the techies say; but by 2020, or 2025, or 2030, there will be more of this than people expect. And that will have some fallout effects.

Let me also amplify on proportional representation. It doesn't really make sense now, but if you do start to get a multiparty system, then you have to think about it. Right after the Canadian elections in 1993, the *Toronto Globe & Mail* said that Canadians had to start thinking about proportional representation, because this chaotic situation and party structure was developing. If that chaos continues, they *will* have to think about it.

What should happen in the United States—and here is yet another reason to think about some proportional representation, cumulative voting, or whatever—also depends on how the courts deal with the questions being drawn into play in terms of racial representation. Some of these systems can be used to give different groups representation without drawing districts that look like spastic octopi. It is just not necessary to do that. Then there is the loss of community in such districts. By the time that much sense of community has been lost, we might as well think about some of the proportional representation. In any event, I think it should be discussed, although nothing should do anything until we have more information.

And if the party system is balkanizing, then I think attention has to return to one of the points that the Committee for the Constitutional System has made in one form or another for some time. This is the idea of having some way to force a national election, if in fact the separated powers do get out of hand. If we had an independent president and a Democratic House and a Republican Senate, that could get kind of unbelievable. We haven't tried that yet; but after what we have now, who is to say it's impossible? If they were all to get into an ideological food fight, it would be useful to have some mechanism that could come into play.

Finally, because technology is going to have a major effect on politics in ways that people do not yet anticipate, we will see systems that enable people to register and vote with much more ease and access—by phones, by touching a screen. There have been tests of voting in a lot of different ways, and some of this is doable. Highly sophisticated identification-type devices are being made by American firms, but not sold much in this country because of constitutional issues in their use. If some of this starts to come into play, we could have many more people voting, especially if there were multiple parties and more issues on the ballot, because these should produce turnout increases too. Suppose this kicked up our turnout to something like 65 to 70 percent, which is Canadian-level turnout? It would probably have a quite substantial impact on our politics, on legislation, and on the party system.

It is important, in considering what is useful and necessary, to try to predict (with the help of analysis in the United States and the other G-7 nations) where these issues are heading in the next five, ten, or fifteen years. Substantial political upheaval and institutional reform appear to be on the horizon.

A Rationale

Donald L. Robinson

We have seen a century-long, worldwide quest for the proper forms of constitutional democracy. I hardly need to underscore the fact that now, living as we do in the wake of the collapse of the Soviet Union. In addition, the nations of South Africa, Japan, Canada, and many others have joined in this quest for the proper forms of constitutional democracy.

Americans know that constitutional form is only part of what is necessary for a viable constitutional system. There are cultural issues that underlie the question of constitutional viability. Indeed, many American social scientists believe that constitutional form is really not very important.

But the Framers of the Constitution knew better, and I think the American people suspect that the form of government is very important. It shapes opportunity, it channels energy, it conditions possibilities. I believe that the condition of our culture now is not unrelated to the matter of our constitutional system and the frustrations it puts in our way.

Take for example the notion that democracy requires strong, competitive parties, the so-called doctrine of a responsible two-party system. It has been held that democracy works best where there is competition between strong parties, and it works best of all in the context of two competitive political parties—one governing, the other providing a useful alternative.

The American constitutional system makes it virtually impossible to have a party system consisting of two strong national parties. Many factors help to frustrate our political parties: the antimajoritarian impulse, and the federal system, based on wariness about power being centralized. But the form of our national constitutional system contributes to it, too. Indeed, our constitutional system both shapes and reflects the cultural values that underlie our constitutional system and helps to keep parties weak and decentralized.

The fact is that the attempt to build strong parties represents an attempt to outwit the Framers of the Constitution. The people sense that, and they resist it. Thus, proposals to channel public financing of political campaigns through the parties is a dog that will not hunt politically, as are calls for ballots that compel straight party-line voting. These ideas fly in the face of the antipartisan impulse that produced the progressive reforms in this country, things like the so-called Australian ballot, nomination by primaries, office block ballots, and so on.

The point of departure for reformers—not just now but throughout American history and I suspect in the foreseeable future—must be people's suspicion and frustration with politics. Popular attitudes, deep and abiding in this culture, support a system that checks power. Public opinion sees advantages in such a system. Unless action is supported by large and durable majorities, it ought not to be taken. Thus, the Madisonian checks curtailed the New Deal and reigned in the Great Society. The same system saved Civil Rights in the 1980s. Now it protects the poor and the vulnerable, as well as the environment, from the mean-spirited and reckless legions in the House of Representatives.

At the same time we need to recognize that the status quo favors the rich and the well born, who are at great advantage by a system that stacks the odds against strong governmental and political action. Thus, when the left, from the 1930s through the 1960s, wanted to enact programs to redistribute wealth and opportunity, the system bent those programs out of shape. Now, when the populist right attempts to act on a presumed mandate to dismantle federal bureaucracy and strengthen the private sector and local governments, inertia again favors the status quo.

The American people generally approve of this moderating tendency of our political system. We want leadership, but we are also suspicious of it, and we resist the plebiscitary presidency.

Lately there is evidence that people may be getting a little impatient with this pattern of our politics. We are no longer as rich a nation as we used to be, comparatively, and we are certainly not as cocky. Our economy looks a little more vulnerable now that the dollar has fallen by 50 percent within five years against the yen; we look and feel vulnerable. Maybe we no longer can count on the abundance of this continent to ensure our position as the number one nation in the world.

Social relations also seem to be posing a more threatening challenge to our system. We wish we could protect our borders against illegal immigration. We are beginning to think we may need a stronger state than we have. At the same time, people want to hold the system more accountable. Of course, such a mood can fuel the politics of paranoia—an antidemocratic or anticonstitutionalist impulse. Thus, it behooves sensible people to ponder these moods and be ready with alternatives if the public begins to sense that panaceas like term limits and the item veto and Balanced Budget Amendments are not going to solve our problems.

Since its founding, the Committee on the Constitutional System has responded to this sense of systemic strain. We were galvanized originally in the beginning of the 1980s by a concern about deficits, which were opposed by everyone, and yet no one seemed to be able to do anything about them; and what was worse, there was no way to hold the government accountable for these deficits. There was a great deal of finger-pointing. The president was blaming Congress, Congress was blaming the president, and they were all blaming the Federal Reserve. There was no way for a voter who was concerned about deficits to punish those responsible.

In addition, we faced recurrent gridlock—a sense of paralysis and corruption, divided government. Thoughtful people banded together in the Committee on the Constitutional System to consider what could be done about these problems. There were relatively few academics involved. It was mostly people with experience in government who came together to form the committee and began to consider changes that were quite radical in the context of American history.

Now I want to relate what we have been doing to the worldwide movement around issues of constitutional form and democracy. Most of the world's constitutional systems have been parliamentary in form during the twentieth century. Many governments in Europe and nations under European influence were in crisis in the post–Second World War period, because they emphasized representation at the expense of authority and coherence and energy in government. Particularly in France and Italy, there was this sense that governments were representative to a fault and often near paralysis because they were unable to mobilize majorities to act.

The need, it was felt, was to strengthen the executive and to make it less vulnerable to majorities in the assemblies. One method was to give the prime minister power of dissolution, a whip hand, particularly in a two-party system. But many parliamentary systems withdrew from that alternative on the ground that strengthening the executive to that extent would make the prime minister too strong and invite extreme oscillations in public policy.

The trick was to keep the assembly representative (usually with a system of proportional representation)—to keep the prime minister on a short leash, vulnerable to motions of no confidence, but at the same time to find a way to give the regime strengthened executive power. The breakthrough, conceptually, came during the 1950s in France, when the Gaullists developed the model of the Fifth French Republic, which added a separately elected president to the parliamentary system of the Fourth Republic. There were other changes, too; but the essential change in the Fifth Republic was to add to the French parliamentary form of government a president, with authority in foreign affairs and able to intervene in emergencies and resolve great difficulties. A president could give government in France coherence, and energy, and the necessary authority to deal with crises.

A variant of the French form is seen in the German Federal Republic. Such "hybrid constitutionalism" (sometimes called "semi-presidentialism") is now the preferred model in Eastern Europe. The Eastern European regimes look not to the United States as the model of constitutional democracy, but instead to France and Germany. When they call on experts to come and offer counsel to them, frequently they seek folks from those Northern and Western European countries, rather than the United States.

The United States is not about to adopt a parliamentary system. We are immunized against it! We want checks and balances for the reasons I indicated earlier. At the same time, we are beginning to recognize that our government needs stronger political controls over the bureaucracy, a greater ability to act, and the voters' ability to hold the government accountable for what it does.

I have come to believe that the process adopted by parliamentary government—to think about what was wrong and adopt an institutional reform that moved it in the direction of the presidential system—is one that we ought to consider here. Perhaps there will be a convergence of constitutional forms. There is a great deal to be said for the accountability that a parliamentary system affords. Yet it lacks coherence and energy. There is much to be said for our system of separated powers, with its checks and balances. What we lack is the ability to hold executive power accountable, so that we can trust it to take leadership.

The reason we are skeptical about presidential leadership is that we are afraid we could not hold it accountable if we unleashed it from the system of separated powers. We will never trust a stronger presidency unless we are assured that we can hold it accountable. This is why, for example, we insist on retaining staggered elections. Staggered elections help to make the power of our system accountable.

One way to strengthen the president (an idea the Committee on the Constitutional System has explored a good deal) would be to coordinate the electoral cycles so that president, House, and Senate would be chosen together every four years. That would help to ensure that the government was empowered over a period of four years to enact a program, based on its electoral campaign. This idea is a good one if what we want to do is unleash presidential power for coherent leadership. But it is greeted with skepticism by the American people, because we are afraid to give presidential leadership so much power. And so, we have not had much luck in the Committee on the Constitutional System selling the idea of coordinated electoral cycles.

We will not have luck with the idea of coordinate electoral cycles until we build into the proposal some way to hold such a government to account, if within that four-year cycle it goes stray or otherwise violates the political promise in America. What we need is a system that would have enabled us, for example, in a year like 1930 or 1931, to judge that the government we put in place in 1928 was on the wrong track and needed to be reorganized.

Constitutional democracy is a quest. The jury is always out. There is certainly little impulse in the country at this time for even mild structural reform. But systems unravel quickly in this world, as we know from what happened to the Soviet Union and from seeing what is happening in Canada, Australia, and South Africa. Who could have predicted what has happened in South Africa?

We may soon, suddenly, want a government that can act—whether for left- or right-wing purposes, whether for communitarian or market-oriented goals. Americans, I trust, will never want direct, untrammeled democracy. The popular impulse must be tempered, and Americans deeply understand that. Until we are assured that referenda, for example, will not carry away our liberties, we are going to resist the impulse to move in the direction of referenda.

At the same time, we must not frustrate democracy overmuch. We need a government that can act effectively, and I hope we will insist on one we can hold accountable.

Government in the Next Century

What the People Want from Government

Patricia McGinnis

The Council for Excellence in Government is a nonprofit, nonpartisan, bipartisan organization whose seven hundred fifty members are leaders in the private sector. All of them have served in government. We think that raising the quality and productivity of the executive-congressional relationship is critical to the future of the federal government and of the country.

Improving the performance of government is in fact the Council's mission. We work on two levels. The first is our involvement in many projects that entail hands-on work with leaders in the executive branch and Congress as well as other levels of government, as well as partnership arrangements that focus on specific management problems or address systemic issues. These projects develop leadership and management skills to produce results. Second, on a broader scale, we are particularly concerned with building public understanding and confidence in government, especially at the federal level.

Recently we worked with Peter Hart and Bob Teeter—the bipartisan pollsters who conduct polls for the *Wall Street Journal* and NBC News, among others—to help us develop a public opinion survey on the role and effectiveness of government. Our goal through this more in-depth survey was to understand what people think government should do, at what level, and how they regard its effectiveness.

We preceded this opinion survey (which was conducted in mid-March among 1,000 citizens, not just voters) with two focus groups where we explored these issues in more depth, in conversation with about two dozen people.

We began by asking participants about their concept of the American dream—a way to frame the discussion that seemed to us to be interesting and important. In one sense, what we found is not surprising at all. People are divided about fifty-fifty on whether the standard of living for their children will be better than their own. A great majority thinks their own standard of living is better than that of their parents.

We also included an open-ended question, without three or four multiple choices (which is unusual for an opinion survey). It produced some interesting results for us. We asked people how they define the American dream. What we heard was a description of a dream that is much less expansive, and much more one of stability and just holding on, than we expected or that would have been expressed by Americans in the past. The dream for most people has changed from one of optimism to one of hoping to hold onto a job, keep a family together, and just preserve the status quo.

What was particularly significant for us was that, by a margin of 56 percent to 31 percent, Americans think that government hinders rather than helps their families in achieving the American dream. By a margin of 72 percent to 21 percent, people said that the federal government creates more problems than it solves; by a margin of 57 percent to 33 percent, they said the same thing about state government. The role of government in the view of these people is therefore highly negative.

The poll confirmed what we already knew about the level of public confidence in government. It is quite low, and the trend over the last twenty years is borne out by our poll. We looked at historical data in framing these questions. Confidence in federal institutions—the executive branch, Congress, and the judiciary—was in the high 40 percent range two decades ago. Now, among other American institutions, only 15 percent of the American people expressed some or a great deal of confidence in the federal government. It is at the bottom of the list.

Just above the federal government's confidence rating is that of the national media, at about 19 percent; I don't believe these two figures are unrelated. Where state and local governments are concerned, there is more confidence, but it is much diminished. Twenty-three percent expressed confidence in state government and 31 percent in local government, down from 50 percent two decades ago.

The poll contains strong messages for those in Congress and the executive branch who are seeking to reshape government. One of them, for example, concerns shifting responsibility from the federal government to the states. Again, in a national opinion survey (and without being able to have an in-depth conversation with each respondent), it is hard to know exactly what this means. But it is clear that people want government closer to them so they can be more involved and hold government more accountable. Seventy-five percent favor giving states more responsibility for programs currently managed at the federal level, even though—and we asked these questions in a number of different ways—most people believe that if responsibility is shifted to state government, their state taxes will increase and their federal taxes will stay the same. Yet even in this circumstance, they favor that sort of shift.

In exploring the reasons for such support, we found that people think both the quality and the fairness in administering programs would improve. One of the reasons why the responsibility for many programs originally shifted from the states to the federal government was to improve the equity and fairness with which they were administered.

The poll also made a strong point about making government more effective through better management, drawing on practices in the private sector such as paying federal employees on the basis of performance and having more flexibility in hiring and firing.

At the end of the poll, we asked people what their main message would be to the federal government and gave them three choices. The message chosen by 50 percent was to make government more effective through better management. Thirty-eight percent would shift more responsibility to states and localities; only 9 percent would make government smaller by cutting programs.

Americans showed throughout the poll that they believe there is an important and strong role for government in a number of areas of our lives. They indicated clearly that they want government to be more responsive and to work for them, and they do not see that happening now. The term "disconnect" has been used a lot recently, and it certainly characterizes the findings in this poll.

Another strong point was that government at all levels should involve citizens in its work. In fact, the numbers really surprised me. Eighty-one percent of those polled favored structural changes to engage people more in government at all levels, rather than having government simply step aside and allow citizens and volunteer groups to become more involved.

The question for the Council for Excellence in Government and for the Committee on the Constitutional System is: what kinds of reforms should be considered to make government more responsive and more accountable to its citizens? The poll suggested giving more responsibility to state and local governments, but not specifically how to go about it. In some of our focus groups, as we talked about that and about the block grant process, we heard participants sound some cautionary notes. Yes, in principle, people want responsibility shifted closer to them; but they want this to be done carefully and thoughtfully. We even heard them say, "Experiment; try something; see how it works."

Americans want greater citizen involvement in almost every policy area that we covered. They want responsibility for each of these issues to be shared not only among levels of government but also between government and individuals and business.

The greater focus in the poll on management and performance and results is unmistakable. At the Council we translate into the public sector context the kind of transformations that we have seen in the private sector. So many companies have radically changed the way they operate and have become more results oriented, largely in response to competitive pressures. But we have also seen some amazing transformations through strong leadership; establishment of clear, measurable goals; flexible and innovative management; a focus on people and performance; and the rewarding of performance.

We think that there should be much greater emphasis in designing legislation and administering programs, particularly at the federal level, on identifying the desired results. A good example is the health goals for the nation that have been set for the year 2000. We should emphasize agreement on reliable measures of performance so that people can be held accountable for results rather than process, and so solutions can be tailored much more innovatively to achieve the desired results.

The specific reforms that might be considered should come out of a better dialogue with the American people—not so-called direct democracy, but real representative government that focuses on the results that people want.

The Contract with America, in my view, had the great value of being a clear public commitment to an agenda—something we seldom see, particularly from Congress. The kind of leadership that people are looking for is a president and congressional leaders who would regularly present a clear articulation of their priorities and specific commitments—agendas could be presented each year or at the beginning of each Congress with regular updates.

Such public communications would provide a basis for negotiation between and within the branches of government. They would allow people to cheer, reject, or help shape the public agenda, but certainly to hold their leaders accountable for results.

Four Challenges to the Political System

Milton D. Morris

I have been impressed with the literature on the need for reform, for change in the political system and the political process, but I am inclined to urge some caution in how we take demands for change, or at least what we see the problem to be, and therefore to fix it.

It is not entirely clear when we talk about a restless public, about some of the public sentiments reflected over the last few years, how much of this represents a developing new challenge in American political life, or merely a slight elevation in an important part of American tradition with respect to politics. My suspicion is that there is less dramatic change and more of an elevation in the expressions of concern than we are inclined to believe.

Moreover, the more I look at public attitudes and public opinion, the more uncertain I am about how to apply any set of polls to thinking about what is wrong or how to go about fixing it.

One of the most consistent points about public opinion polls in the last few years on these subjects, as well as about the behavior of the electorate, is volatility. The surveys reveal some persisting themes that ought to cause concern about the character and performance of government, but they also show a number of contradictions that require careful sorting out. I am not quite sure we have managed to do that in a way that gives us confidence that we understand the public mood and are ready to address it.

There are no perfect or even near-perfect political systems, and so on any given day we do face structural problems, which contribute to public disenchantment and dissatisfaction with the performance of government.

Yet I hope that we will not rest too heavily on the structural interpretation of our problems. There are structural problems within the political parties, or with the separation of powers, that we can fix and, in doing so, regain overwhelming public support and public confidence and trust in government. But my sense is there is much less to the structural emphasis than meets the eye.

The American political system and our political institutions have been changing rather consistently over time. One of the great achievements of the last three or four decades has been the change in voting and representation that has facilitated considerably greater inclusion in the political system. Not just the voting rights laws but the overall thinking about what fair representation means has been evolving.

While we still have "two political parties," Democratic and Republican, those parties themselves have been undergoing almost continuous change. In the Democratic Party, dramatic changes have occurred in the processes of recruitment, delegate selection, and representation. The Republican Party remains the same in formal structure, but it is profoundly changed in philosophy and outlook from what it was two or three decades ago.

These changes may not be dramatic or forceful enough to be persuasive to the public, but they are significant. And as I look toward the future I expect to see more of that kind of evolution taking place rather than rapid or major systemic change.

Four factors challenge us today as we look at the problems of governance.

First is a growing clash between radical libertarian values on the one hand and traditional democratic values on the other. The desire to be "free"—to be independent of government and/or authority and control—is being reasserted in a variety of ways and circumstances. We hear about eroding freedoms at a time when some might argue we have more freedom than any society has ever had. We hear echoes of that in some of the debates about tax policy: people who now passionately believe their money is theirs and is being confiscated by the government. This challenge will have to be faced direcly as we look over the horizon into the new century.

Second is the explosive growth in technology and information that is transforming decisionmaking and representation—indeed, entire processes of governance. Showers of faxes rain down every day from the White House and from organizations of all kinds, as well as individuals, who are now inserting themselves into decisionmaking processes in ways that were not at all a part of the political equation only a short time ago. In this category too is the ability of the president and every member of Congress to wake up to new polls each day, telling them what the public thinks about virtually every issue.

And of course this flow of information—its volume and density—is a major challenge to the public, the policymakers, and therefore to the system, to sort out and cope with. To assess just how enormous this explosion is, count the number of think tanks that have gone into business over the last decade or two, all pouring out specialized information of various kinds in the policy arena.

Third is the strain, the impact, of diversity on democracy. Our society has perhaps done as well as any in coping with diversity—racial, ethnic, and cultural. Yet the enormous challenges to our political systems created by the range and breadth of diversity in America have still not been adequately met.

Fourth is the challenge of growing economic inequality and diminishing expectation of prosperity. As a society or as a political system, we have not solved the problem of equitably distributing wealth or opportunity. Most of the developed countries—certainly led by the United States—have experienced in recent years an unsettling growth in inequality of income and of wealth, and an increase in the large segment of the population is left feeling pessimistic about the prospects for economic well-being. Democracy does well when people have high expectations and aspirations. Democracy suffers when expectations about achievement and success begin to waver.

These challenges, I think, contribute much more than structural problems or flaws do to the difficulties we now perceive in the political system. And, as we move into the future, our political system will be seeking to adapt in a variety of ways to these and other kinds of pressures. These adaptations are come more through rolling reforms than through formalized structural change.

The System is
Self-Correcting

Bill Frenzel

As a recovering member of the U.S. House of Representatives who has not quite recovered yet, I am going to be quite subjective in my contribution.

First, I must say that I am an incurable optimist. It would be impossible for someone to serve in the House of Representatives in the minority for twenty years without being some kind of cockeyed optimist. But I have never worried about the United States government, nor about the ability of the people of the United States to solve its, or their, problem. And I do not worry about them now. Nor do I think the problems that face this country, systemic or substantive, put us in any kind of crisis.

Second, as to the theory of gridlock, there are some of us who think gridlock is the best thing since indoor plumbing. Gridlock is a natural gift the Framers of our Constitution gave us so that the country would not be subjected to policy swings resulting from the whimsy of the public. And the competition—whether multibranch, multilevel, or multihouse—is important to those checks and balances and to our ongoing kind of centrist government. Thank heaven we do not have a government that nationalizes this year and privatizes next year, and so on ad infinitum.

If we wanted a government that could stand dynamic transcending leadership, we could get ourselves a parliament and a prime minister. We have not wanted that kind of government. Our Framers gave us a government built in the depths of distrust of government. They gave us a government that could not give us more than very little government.

And I suspect that, other than the Swiss, we have probably been rewarded as well as any country with very small amounts of government. I do not mind gridlock. I think the country knows when it needs a change and will call for it, so I do not wring my hands over the problem of gridlock.

As Lloyd Cutler tells us, when we try to reform our government for moral reasons—for faith and morals, or ethical cleanliness, or whatever—we almost always screw it up. The executive branch now consists of only two types of people: advance men and women from the last campaign, and former congressional staffers. They are the only people who can get through the conflict of interest, revolving doors, and disclosure statutes and regulations that Congress and each succeeding administration have passed.

So if you want people with exceedingly little achievement in their lives and little breadth of experience, then you certainly want to write laws based on perfect cleanliness and flawless moral values and keep those laws enforced. But if you want people in the public service who have had broad experience in the professions, or in business, or in education, then maybe you will want to repeal some of those so-called ethical restrictions. My guess is that they will be much harder to take off than they were to put on, which is why I am always nervous about reform. When people talk about change I can barely stomach it; but if they call it reform, you know damned well they are going to stick it to you.

The other thing I have noticed in my experience in politics is that the system is often self-correcting. If there is something wrong that actually impedes a popular policy, a way will be found to get around it. If we have to have trade policies voted on by Congress (and we do), and yet they are subject to filibuster, we will enact a law that makes the filibuster ineffective in voting on the results of trade negotiating authority.

There is always a way to get around the problem. And those who wring their hands in anguish over gridlock are simply the losers. They are the same guys who sit around the card table and scream "deal" because they lost the last hand. In the United States we have a theory of the concurrent majority. This means that very little major policy change is ever made without at least the tacit consent of all the parties to the argument, whether they are political parties, or farmers and city dwellers, or whoever. I like that theory. It works well, and regularly, for us.

Our next worry is whether the people are disaffected with their government. From my experience in elected politics at local, state, and federal levels over three decades, there has never been a time when anyone liked his or her government. As I read history, I do not remember many great heroes in American history; at least they were not great until they died and were beatified by later generations. We never elevate them to herohood, nor name schools after them, nor raise statues to them, until they are gone. While they live, they are just politicians.

The public does not like government. It is never going to like government. It probably should not. Like the relationship between politicians and the press, the public has always viewed its government with a healthy degree of skepticism. A grudging respect? Perhaps. But that respect has to be won with every vote on every single issue. And often the best votes, which should earn respect, are the ones the public hates.

Everyone tells us how disaffected we are. The word "disconnect" does not bother me. The only way I measure disconnection is by whether the public does or does not vote. We were on a downhill glide in voter participation in both congress and presidential elections from 1960 until 1992 and 1994, when we had a slight upturn. That was the time, of course, when members of Congress began wringing their hands, saying "People don't trust us; they don't like us."

I hope the 1992 and 1994 elections are not just an upturn but the beginning of a trend. But if they are not and voting rates continue to fall, the public can simply look in the mirror to place blame.

I do not mean to suggest that we should not fix things if they are broke. The conference behind this book was designed to generate all kinds of ideas. We hope they filter out into the political system and that some of them get picked up, because some are excellent. But if there is one thing polls tell you, it is that your own impressions of public opinion are invariably correct. I used to poll a lot when I was in politics. Usually my polls were the cheapest available, but occasionally we would throw caution to the wind and hire somebody exceptional. The results were always pretty much the same. If we asked the questions in the right way, we could make sure that my electorate supported me right down the line.

Polls are polls. They tell you what people are reacting to the questions you ask at the moment you ask them. Unless you study millions of people, it is hard to find trends or to get solid evidence of where the United States is going.

One thing we do know: every pollster who is any good, and even the ones that are not, will tell you that the American electorate is not volatile. Americans are centrist folks. When Ronald Reagan gets elected we move an inch to the right. When Bill Clinton gets elected we move an inch to the left. When the Democrats are in control of Congress, we are a little left of the center line; and now Newt Gingrich is in. That is our system, so do not expect the electorate to go rushing off in any one direction.

Right now the electorate has not turned stone conservative. It has moved a little to the right, but mostly it was rejecting the Democrats in Congress rather than embracing the Republicans. Surely it had little idea what was in the Contract with America. The media either ignored the Contract or heaped vituperation on it, so that nobody out there had any idea what it was. That, of course, was lucky for Newt, because he could use it as the glue to hold his group together without protest.

Devolution is part of the Republican Contract. Devolution is one of those things we should practice first, or do a little testing of, before we lay it on the subgovernments. I wonder how brave those governors of our states are going to be when we go into recession and the states dependent on the income tax begin to lose revenue. Guess where they are going to come to ask for more federal money.

The only way we can underestimate or denigrate our government is to believe it can do everything for us. Our government, over the years, has proved to be an excellent crisis manager. If we are in war or depression, it does a fairly good job of trying to extricate us. But as a routine manager, forget it. It has the sensitivity of the Internal Revenue Service and the efficiency of the Postal Service. Nobody has a high expectation for it, nor should they.

Some of the contributors to this book write about the disintegration or withering away of the parties. My own judgment is that for at least two decades the Republican Party has been way to the right of the average Republican voter, and the Democratic Party has been way to the left of the average Democratic voter. This can be confirmed by voting patterns in Congress, or by political party platforms produced quadrennially.

Both parties and their congressional incumbents appear to have decided they want a parliamentary or Westminster kind of system. But our system is our own, and it is regional rather than totally partisan. My guess is the parties are going to sink lower before they get better. I only hope they get better soon.

Let's Eliminate the Midterm Election

James L. Sundquist

Amid all the discussion of just what the 1994 midterm election wrought, a more basic question needs to be asked: Would the U.S. government have worked better in 1993 and 1994, and would it be working better in 1995 and 1996, if the midterm election had never been held at all?

The Committee on the Constitutional System, which was formed in 1981 by an impressive group of elder statesmen, could not agree on most of the proposals for fundamental constitutional change that is considered—except for one. That was to eliminate the congressional election that is held at the midpoint of every presidential term. The committee proposed to accomplish that by lengthening the terms of members of the House of Representatives to four years, their terms to be concurrent with that of the president, and extending Senate terms to eight years, with half the members to be chosen at each presidential election.

The result would be to give a newly chosen government four years to accomplish what it promised in its campaign to do—to carry out its mandate, whatever that might be—before its elected members again had to face the voters.

(As an alternative to lengthening the Senate terms from the present six to eight years, the same objective could be accomplished by shortening the term to four. The Committee preferred the eight-year term, partly out of respect for the Framers' concept that the Senate should be a more stable body than the House, less subject to transient moods in the electorate, and partly because of the supposition that senators would be more likely to support the proposal.)

Lengthening the House term is a very old idea. No other advanced country in the world has so short a term for its legislative body. One or two countries have three-year terms, but most have four years or, as in the case of Britain, five. The Convention of 1787 did consider a longer term for House members—as well as a shorter one—before settling rather arbitrarily on two years. The question has been raised from time to time since then. In 1906 the House approved a constitutional amendment to extend its members' terms to four years, but the Senate did not take kindly to the measure, partly because it contained no provision to prevent House members from challenging senators at the mid-point of the former's new terms. (More recent proposals for four-year House terms would require that representatives resign their seats if they chose to run for the Senate at midterm.)

The most serious effort came in the late 1960s, when President Lyndon Johnson sent a special message to Congress proposing four-year House terms, concurrent with the president's. The proposition aroused great controversy in the House, the details of which are recounted in Charles O. Jones's book entitled *Every Second Year,* and the amendment never emerged from committee. While the members initially responded favorably to the idea in principle, as might be expected, they could never agree on exactly what form the plan should take, and—since it was Lyndon Johnson who had suggested giving them this goodie—they were deeply suspicious that there must be a joker in it somewhere.

But the year 1995 is certainly an appropriate time to reopen the question. The 1994 midterm election was assuredly a fateful one. It replaced a unified Democratic government with one divided between the parties, which means that anything to be accomplished must come through the ordeal of bipartisan compromise. And it shifted much of the responsibility for program initiative from the president to Congress, which has proven historically to be too decentralized and individualistic to serve well as the fount of national leadership.

Democrats will surely agree, instantaneously, that they would be better off if the 1994 election had never happened. To begin with, more of them would still have their seats in Congress, but the issue is much broader than that. Democrats can argue that if President Clinton tackled the difficult problems facing the nation, and laid out the kind of ambitious program that those problems demanded, and then had to get it all accomplished in time to face the voters in just twenty-one months, he was fated from the outset to lose.

What chance did President Clinton really have?

First of all, the twenty-one months have to be reduced by the length of time it takes to get a new government organized. Perhaps, because of Bill Clinton's personal idiosyncracies and managerial habits, it took him longer than necessary. Granted, he made the same mistake that Jimmy Carter made in surrounding himself with cronies from his own state and his campaign apparatus who lacked experience in Washington and background for grappling with complex national and international problems. But in the best of circumstances, it is a slow and ponderous process to assemble a White House staff and a cabinet and to appoint several hundred other key officeholders, particularly if a president is trying to diversify the government and not merely dip into the same old pool. The background checks alone can be excruciatingly time-consuming.

Robert Reischauer gives his considered judgment that no matter how quickly the Clinton administration had gotten organized, and no matter how expeditiously it had proceeded, health care reform never could have been accomplished within the two-year limit. It was far too complex, affected far too many interests that had to be heard and accommodated, and contained too many innovations that had to be resolved in intensive national debate. If Clinton had had four years instead of two as his time horizon, he could have prepared his plan less hastily, taken ample time to explain it, and still have perhaps enough time left for discussion, negotiation, and amendment. Perhaps the whole idea would have died anyway, for all the reasons Robin Toner has suggested, but perhaps not. At least, it would not have been doomed from the beginning. But even if he got nowhere on health care, he would have had time to exert leadership in the area of perhaps the greatest public disenchantment with government—that of welfare reform, which he promised in his campaign to tackle but could never get around to in the midst of the tumultuous health care debate.

Yet even sadder is Reischauer's comment that Clinton did the right thing on the deficit—that it was necessary to set fiscal policy on a more prudent course in the interest of the country, that by taking unpopular measures he did succeed in cutting the deficit by 40 percent, but that his courage contributed heavily to the 1994 defeat of the Democratic party. As Reischauer put it, "No good deed goes unpunished." As he observed, George Bush, likewise punished for raising taxes, can surely sympathize.

But suppose President Clinton had had two extra years to live his good deed down. Short-run pain can be overcome by longer-term gains. By 1996 the voters' resentment would have faded, their attention would have turned to other things, and if cutting the deficit did succeed in improving the economy, the longer-term gains of the president's fiscal policy might have begun to be realized. The experience of Margaret Thatcher in Britain is pertinent. Immediately on taking office, she dealt with her country's comparable fiscal problem, and some other problems as well, by passing some highly unpopular measures. But she had five years to live down her austerity program, the necessity for it came to be understood, and the benefits began to re realized. When the fifth year came around, she was rewarded with a big reelection majority, and she won still another election victory after that.

Moreover, just as we have to subtract from the beginning of Clinton's two years the time it takes to get the government organized, we have to deduct from the other end the time that can be rendered unavailable if any significant group, or even sometimes a single individual, chooses to use all of the delaying tactics that are available in the legislative process. The nearer the second year of a Congress approaches its close, the more the power of opponents of any measure is enhanced. This is especially true in the Senate where, since the recent rediscovery of Rule 22, it has become routine for a minority of 41 members—41 percent of the body—to block any bill it dislikes by refusing to limit debate. In both houses, bills can be held in committee until a time too late for floor action, and even if similar measures are passed in both houses, they can die through failure of conference committees to agree. Thus the short two-year life of a Congress, with its abrupt and prescheduled end, works against leadership by any president and strengthens his congressional opponents—whether one sees those opponents as obstructionists or as modern Horatios staving off catastrophe.

So, to the Democrats, it must seem clear that they would have been, and would be now, better off if the midterm election had never been held. That election simply set them too short a deadline. In four years, they could have made a better record to run on in 1996 and, what is more important, accomplished more for the country.

But what of the Republicans? I think a strong case can be made that they too would be better off if there had been no 1994 election. True, they gained a smashing victory, and their spirits are high. But, by 1996, will they have maintained their position or lost ground?

Like the Democrats in 1993, the Republicans in 1995 have a mandate problem. They asked for power in the midterm election, made promises—uniquely formalized in their Contract with America—yet the obstacles in their way are at least as formidable as those Bill Clinton faced two years before. Like him, they are granted less than two years before their time is up and they have to present their achievements for approval of the voters. And they must do so under the great handicap of trying to lead the country from Capitol Hill. Uniting the Congress is always daunting—first, because it is divided into two often competing and jealous bodies, and, second, because each of those is in turn decentralized into committees that represent separate, again often competing and jealous, centers of power. The competition in this Congress will be intensified as the race for the party's presidential nomination heats up, with candidates who are members of Congress trying to demonstrate their leadership capacity by pulling the party in different directions, and candidates outside Congress intervening in the debate as well. In these two years, it seems unlikely that Senator Dole will set out to make a hero of Newt Gingrich by following his leadership—or vice versa. And even when the Republicans on Capitol Hill are able to agree on a particular policy, they must confront a president who will be using whatever political skill he can muster to keep them from achieving anything that they can exploit in the 1996 campaign—provided, of course, that in blocking their initiatives he can avoid painting himself as the obstructionist responsible for gridlock.

The result by 1996 could well be a shambles, marked by the "pile of vetoes" that Clinton has insisted he is trying to avoid but will find unavoidable, in which no party will emerge looking good. The voters of 1996 may well be as disappointed in the Republican performance as those of 1994 were disenchanted by Bill Clinton's. The two parties are already so discredited that a majority of the electorate tells pollsters that it would like to see a third party come into being. By the end of 1996, the gridlock—and the constant bickering and recrimination—cannot but alienate the voters even more.

It seems significant that Republican National Chairman Haley Barbour, as early as the spring of 1995, was already warning the country not to expect too much from his triumphant party. They would be obstructed at every step by the Democratic president, he cautioned, preparing his alibi well in advance. He did not, of course, refer to the problem of attaining consensus among the competing leaders and ideological factions within the GOP.

People ask, "Why can't those politicians in Washington just rise above politics, stop their feuding, and get together to do what is best for the country?" But they feud not because they are by nature quarrelsome. Successful politicians, of all people, are the ones most likely to have achieved their success by being cordial, conciliatory, genial. They quarrel because they have genuine, deeply held, divergent beliefs, and most of today's politicians entered politics out of zeal to advance their principles. So they are reluctant and slow to "get together" with the opposition, as the people want, because that means yielding on principle and compromising. And, ironically, the same voters who demand that their leaders set aside their differences and act together also tell the pollsters that they respect politicians who "stand up for their principles," and they disdain the waverers who shift their positions according to the prevailing political winds.

So if, at the end of 1996, not one but both parties will have failed to make a record because the unity of the government was destroyed by the midterm election, it follows that both parties—not just the Democrats—would have been better off if that midterm election had not been held. The Democrats would have been fully responsible for their four-year record and could be held fully accountable. If, as they believe, that record would have been a creditable one, they would deserve, and get, another mandate from the people. But if, as the Republicans contend, the Democrats through ineptitude, folly, and blundering would have led the country in the wrong direction, the Republicans would get a vote of confidence in 1996 as strong as the one they received in 1994, but this time that vote would install a unified Republican government—a Republican Congress led by a Republican president—that would have the capacity to attain truly heroic goals. If the current two years of divided government turn out to discredit both parties, then, they may deny the Republicans their opportunity, just as the 1994 election prematurely deprived the Democrats of theirs.

Two years ago, I was advocating the creation of an official blue-ribbon body patterned after the first Hoover commission of the 1940s—which is everybody's model for an eminent, above-politics group of statesmen—to look at the relations between the executive and legislative branches and the entire range of problems arising from the governmental structure that was established in the eighteenth century and has remained fundamentally unchanged. At that time, I was most concerned with the problem of divided government. That is no less a concern today. But now I would propose to elevate to the top of the agenda of such a commission the question of whether the midterm election—which historically has rarely strengthened the government but has repeatedly undermined the presidential leadership on which successful governance depends—should not simply be abolished, to give our government a life span as long, and an opportunity for accomplishment as great, as those of other countries.